Literacy 2.0

Reading and Writing in 21st Century Classrooms

NANCY **FREY** • DOUGLAS **FISHER** • ALEX **GONZALEZ**

Solution Tree | Press

a division of
Solution Tree

555 North Morton Street
Bloomington, IN 47404
800.733.6786 (toll free) / 812.336.7700
FAX: 812.336.7790

email: info@solution-tree.com
solution-tree.com

Visit **go.solution-tree.com/literacy** for live links to the websites mentioned in this book.

Printed in the United States of America

14 13 12 11 10   1 2 3 4 5

FSC
Mixed Sources
Product group from well-managed
forests and other controlled sources
Cert no. SW-COC-002283
www.fsc.org
© 1996 Forest Stewardship Council

Library of Congress Cataloging-in-Publication Data

Frey, Nancy, 1959-
  Literacy 2.0 : reading and writing in 21st century classrooms / Nancy Frey, Douglas Fisher, Alex Gonzalez.
      p. cm.
  Includes bibliographical references and index.
  ISBN 978-1-935249-80-1 (perfect bound) -- ISBN 978-1-935249-81-8 (library edition)
1. Computers and literacy. 2. Education--Effect of technological innovations on. 3. Curriculum planning. I. Fisher, Douglas, 1965- II. Gonzalez, Alex. III. Title.
  LC149.5.F745 2010
  428.0078'54678--dc22
                            2010010180

Solution Tree
Jeffrey C. Jones, CEO & President

Solution Tree Press
President: Douglas M. Rife
Publisher: Robert D. Clouse
Vice President of Production: Gretchen Knapp
Managing Production Editor: Caroline Wise
Senior Production Editor: Risë Koben
Proofreader: David Eisnitz
Text and Cover Designer: Amy Shock

Acknowledgments

Solution Tree Press would like to thank the following reviewers:

Sue Abrams
Literacy Coach
Hopkins Elementary School
Littleton, Colorado

Robert Baroz
English/Language Arts Teacher,
  Grades 6–8
Curley K–8 School
Boston, Massachusetts

Donna Baumbach
Professor Emerita
University of Central Florida
Orlando, Florida

Monica Beane
Assistant Director, Office of
  Instruction
West Virginia Department of
  Education
Charleston, West Virginia

Erica Boling
Assistant Professor, Department of
  Learning and Teaching
Rutgers University
New Brunswick, New Jersey

Meg Ormiston
Professional Development Specialist
Tech Teachers, Inc.
Burr Ridge, Illinois

Michelle Pacansky-Brock
Co-owner and Educational
  Consultant
Teaching Without Walls
San Jose, California

Timothy Shanahan
Director
Center for Literacy
University of Illinois at Chicago

Ashlie Thomas
Language Arts Department Head
Emporia High School
Emporia, Kansas

Nicole Welding
Teacher, Grade 8
Freedom Elementary School
Buckeye, Arizona

Visit **go.solution-tree.com/literacy** for live links to
the websites mentioned in this book.

Table of Contents

About the Authors

Nancy Frey, Ph.D., is a professor of literacy in the School of Teacher Education at San Diego State University (SDSU). She is the recipient of the 2008 Early Career Achievement Award from the National Reading Conference and a Christa McAuliffe Award for excellence in teacher education from the American Association of State Colleges and Universities. She has published in *The Reading Teacher, Journal of Adolescent and Adult Literacy, English Journal, Voices in the Middle, Middle School Journal, Remedial and Special Education,* and *Educational Leadership.* She is a coauthor of the books *Checking for Understanding: Formative Assessment Techniques for Your Classroom, Better Learning Through Structured Teaching: A Framework for the Gradual Release of Responsibility,* and *Content-Area Conversations: How to Plan Discussion-Based Lessons for Diverse Language Learners.* She teaches a variety of courses in SDSU's teacher-credentialing program on elementary and secondary reading instruction and literacy in content areas, classroom management, and supporting students with diverse learning needs. Nancy also teaches classes at Health Sciences High and Middle College in San Diego, where she learns every day from her students and colleagues.

Douglas Fisher, Ph.D., is a professor of language and literacy education in the Department of Teacher Education at San Diego State University and a classroom teacher at Health Sciences High and Middle College. He is the recipient of an International Reading Association Celebrate Literacy Award, the Farmer Award for excellence in writing from the National Council of Teachers of English, and a Christa McAuliffe Award for excellence in teacher education. He has published numerous articles on reading and literacy, differentiated instruction, and curriculum design, as well as books, including *Creating Literacy-Rich Schools for Adolescents* (with Gay Ivey), *Checking for Understanding: Formative Assessment Techniques for Your Classroom* (with Nancy Frey), *Better Learning Through Structured Teaching: A Framework for the Gradual Release of Responsibility* (with Nancy Frey), *Teaching English Language Learners: A Differentiated Approach* (with Carol Rothenberg), and *In a Reading State of Mind: Brain Research, Teacher Modeling, and Comprehension Instruction* (with Nancy Frey and Diane Lapp).

Alex Gonzalez is the technology coordinator at Health Sciences High and Middle College in San Diego. He received an associate degree in computer networking in 2006 and a dual bachelor of science degree in computer networking and network security from Coleman University, San Diego, in 2009. In his approach to the use of technology in the classroom, Alex emphasizes forward thinking, convenience, security, and application. He currently resides in San Diego, where he spends his spare time writing and performing music.

Introduction

2.0 Learning in a 1.0 Classroom

Literacy 2.0 represents a shift, not a replacement. Whereas literacy 1.0 was about access to information, literacy 2.0 is about finding, using, producing, and sharing information. The audience is now the world, and students expect to collaborate, interact, and participate with others across time and space. With these developments have come demands for high levels of proficiency. When a student posts on a blog or updates her website or produces a song for sale on MySpace, the world can comment, and students quickly find out when they make grammatical, spelling, or conceptual errors. In fact, our experience suggests that students are paying more attention to the basic components of literacy and numeracy because of their own increased presence on the public stage.

Literacy 2.0 doesn't make literacy 1.0 obsolete. Similar to new versions of software programs, literacy 2.0 builds on the operating system of literacy 1.0. Literacy 2.0 assumes that students learn vocabulary, comprehension, creative and critical thinking, writing, and so on but that they do so in different venues. In other words, literacy 2.0 is the next version of literacy, rather than an update. And literacy 2.0 requires knowledge of 21st century skills, especially those related to collaboration, creativity, listening and viewing, and sharing, locating, and storing information.

Increasingly, middle and high school students are using their literacies in service of other purposes. Both in school and outside of it, adolescents are applying what they know about literacy 1.0 in new ways as new technologies become available to them. Yet in many cases, it is not enough for students to rely on what they have learned from traditional literacy instruction. Although many adolescents take pride in being early adopters of new tools, they may lack the ability to locate and evaluate information, or they may share it in ways that are inaccurate and inadequate.

Technology Moves Into the Core Curriculum

The need for literate members of the 21st century has been stated in count-less ways. Some stress that a global society requires sophisticated consumers and creators of information. Others talk of the risk to societies when users have access to information but not the analytical skills necessary for evaluat-ing whether it is truthful or not. Still others worry about the prevalence of the unquestioning belief that "if it's on the Internet, it must be true."

Professional organizations such as the International Reading Association (IRA), the National Council of Teachers of English (NCTE), and the Inter-national Society for Technology in Education (ISTE) recognize and empha-size that the dividing line between literacy and technology has dissolved. For example, the NCTE has determined that 21st century readers and writers need to be able to:

- Develop proficiency with the tools of technology;
- Build relationships with others to pose and solve problems collabora-tively and cross-culturally;
- Design and share information for global communities to meet a variety of purposes;
- Manage, analyze, and synthesize multiple streams of simultaneous information;
- Create, critique, analyze, and evaluate multi-media texts; and
- Attend to the ethical responsibilities required by these complex envi-ronments. (National Council of Teachers of English, 2009, p. 15)

Similarly, the ISTE has developed National Educational Technology Stan-dards that address "what students should know and be able to do to learn effec-tively and live productively in an increasingly digital world." The standards focus on:

- Creativity and Innovation
- Communication and Collaboration
- Research and Information Fluency
- Critical Thinking, Problem Solving, and Decision Making
- Digital Citizenship
- Technology Operations and Concepts (International Society for Technology in Education, 2007)

The educational assessment field has also acknowledged that the ability to access, analyze, and produce information for a digital society is an essen-tial 21st century skill. The National Assessment of Educational Progress (NAEP), informally called "the Nation's Report Card," is developing a test of technological literacy that will be administered beginning in 2012. A draft framework for the assessment, which will form the basis for what is tested, identifies three categories of "cross-cutting practices" that "a technologically literate person should be able to apply" and gives examples of each:

Identifying and Applying Principles

- Understands the nature of technology in its broadest sense.

- Is aware of the various digital tools and their appropriateness for different tasks.

- Knows how technology is created and how it shapes society and in turn is shaped by society.

- Understands basic engineering concepts and terms, such as systems, constraints, and trade-offs.

- Understands cultural differences by engaging with learners of other cultures.

Using Processes to Solve Problems and Achieve Goals

- Uses a wide range of technological tools and systems, ranging from kitchen appliances and alarm clocks to cars, computers, communication devices, and the Internet.

- Can apply technological concepts and abilities creatively, including those of engineering design and information technology, to solve problems and meet goals.

- Collects and analyzes data to develop a solution and complete a project.

- Uses multiple processes and diverse perspectives to explore alternative solutions.

- Can evaluate claims and make intelligent decisions.

Communicating and Collaborating

- Communicates information and ideas effectively to multiple audiences using a variety of media and formats.

- Participates thoughtfully and productively in discussing critical societal issues involving technology related to humans, the environment, knowledge, and citizenship.

- Collaborates with peers and experts. (WestEd, 2009, pp. 1-7–1-8)

The NAEP technological literacy assessment promises to feature different types of items, including extended-response items that measure a range of skills. For example, students "might be asked to construct a wind turbine from a set of virtual components in which there are several combinations of turbine blades and generators." The students would need to test different combinations, record data from their tests, and "select different types of graphic representations for the tabulated data they captured. . . . Finally, the students could be asked to interpret their data, make a recommendation for the best combination of turbine blade and generator, and justify their choice in a short written (typed) response" (WestEd, 2009, pp. 4-6–4-7). Consider the myriad skills needed to answer this item. Knowledge of science and mathematics are certainly key, but the task also requires the literacy skills needed to predict, confirm, monitor, evaluate, and justify.

The standards of the various professional organizations and the proposed NAEP assessment are nothing less than a clarion call—learning in the 21st century can no longer be limited to mimicking existing knowledge. But the question is whether students' curricular and instructional experiences are preparing them to function at higher cognitive levels.

Travels in Time

In 1895, with the publication of *The Time Machine*, H. G. Wells introduced the world to a new device in literature, time travel. Well over one hundred years and countless books, movies, TV shows, and comics later, time travel is widely accepted as a tool that writers can use to make their point. As Wells started the journey, so do we:

> The Time Traveller (for so it will be convenient to speak of him) was expounding a recondite matter to us. His grey eyes shone and twinkled, and his usually pale face was flushed and animated. The fire burned brightly, and the soft radiance of the incandescent lights in the lilies of silver caught the bubbles that flashed and passed in our glasses. Our chairs, being his patents, embraced and caressed us rather than submitted to be sat upon, and there was that luxurious after-dinner atmosphere when thought roams gracefully free of the trammels of precision. And he put it to us in this way—marking the points with a lean forefinger—as we sat and lazily admired his earnestness over this new paradox (as we thought it) and his fecundity. (Wells, 1895/1995, p. 1)

But the time traveler in our story is different. He's a student from 1895, the same year that Wells published his book, and he has been transported to 2010. Emerging from the time machine, our traveler is bewildered. Looking for a horse and buggy to take him to the store to trade for some needed goods, he realizes that transportation is vastly different from what he is used to. When he finally finds a store, he isn't sure what he's looking at. The supplies he needs are covered in a strange material (which we call plastic), and he isn't sure how to get to the food inside. Assuming that the covering is edible, our time traveler ingests the plastic and subsequently needs medical attention.

Visiting a doctor is an unforgettable experience for him. While there are familiar aspects to it, such as meeting with an expert and getting advice from this person, the machines all around him are strange and cold and scary. Sounds and lights are emitted, but he can't make sense of any of it.

Upon leaving the clinic, our time traveler stumbles into a school. While the clothes on the people in the building are different from what he's used to, entering a classroom is a calming experience. There are rows of desks and an adult up front talking and writing on a board. The board looks a little different (his was black, and this one is white), but the teaching style is familiar. So is the behavior of several students in the class: some are sleeping, and others are talking quietly to one another while the teacher repeats himself, asking questions that he already knows the answer to. The ones in the front of the class are a bit more conscious of their outward appearance, so instead they adopt the vacant stare usually reserved for daydreaming. Maybe they are time traveling, too, wishing they were in the near future, when this class will be over. Our time traveler breathes a sigh of relief because he is finally on familiar ground. This classroom differs little from the one he left behind.

We are less comforted.

Considering all the advances that have occurred in the last 115 years, it is disturbing that education has changed so little. Beyond the superficial alterations, much remains the same. The teacher stands in front of the room, lecturing about content the students are supposed to know, while the students are expected to passively absorb all the information. In fact, that's an even more ancient belief—John Locke first forwarded the notion of *tabula rasa* (blank slate) in 1690. (It should be noted that we were able to locate the information contained in that last sentence in seconds using Wikipedia.) Good behavior is measured in large part by how quiet and still the students remain, a highly unnatural state for most adolescents. What is even more discouraging is that if they were anywhere but in a traditional classroom, they would be searching for information, communicating with others about it, and synthesizing it in order to create something new. Yet despite the acknowledged importance of interactive and dynamic learning, one can witness little of it in traditional secondary classrooms. Instead, many teachers teach as they themselves were taught—through a transmission model. In other words, sit still, be quiet, and I'll tell you what you need to know. It's 1895 all over again.

Moving Into the 21st Century Skills Mindset

Today's students have a deep-seated need to communicate and collaborate, to access information at any time of the day or night, and to have the tools that will enable them to synthesize, evaluate, and create information. In 2009, the Speak Up project surveyed more than 280,000 middle and high school students and asked them how they would use money from the federal stimulus package to improve their schools. The students responded in the following ways:

- Fifty-two percent recommended a laptop for each student.
- Fifty-one percent asked for more games and simulations for teaching concepts.
- Forty-four percent requested the use of digital media tools.
- Forty-three percent said they would install interactive whiteboards.
- Forty-two percent wanted online textbooks.
- Forty percent stated that email, instant messaging, and text messaging tools would enhance their learning. (Speak Up, 2009)

There are a number of ways that we can move into the 21st century skills mindset and meet our students. An important part of that shift is understanding that literacy functions remain the same while the tools have changed.

It's time for a confession. We feel stressed trying to keep up with the innovations in the 21st century. Not too long ago, we were asked to join a Ning, and we didn't know what it was. The first time a student wanted to tweet us, we had not yet heard of Twitter and didn't know what that meant. Our stress was reduced when we heard Marc Prensky, in his 2008 keynote at the National Council of Teachers of English conference, suggest that we stop thinking of technology in terms of nouns (PowerPoint, YouTube, or Twitter) and instead think in terms of verbs (presenting, sharing, and communicating). In other words, we should focus on the functions of the technology rather than the tools or forms of technology. Thankfully, the functions are familiar. Importantly, we'll never keep up with all of the tools (forms). We just need to understand the functions for which the tools are developed so that we can be smart consumers and pick and choose the tools that serve our instructional needs. Realizing that was a liberating and stress-reducing experience.

Mark Weiser (1991, p. 94) observed, "The most profound technologies are those that disappear—they weave themselves into the fabric of everyday life until they are indistinguishable from it." Like the chalkboards of our time traveler's school days, the best technologies fade into the background. The tools themselves evolve; our task as educators is to foreground the communication while keeping abreast of the technologies that support it. If we focus on the tool but lose sight of the purpose, we are forever condemned to playing catch-up in a rapidly changing technology landscape. Remember beepers? They enjoyed a brief popularity in the 1990s but became obsolete with the widespread use of cell phones. Few people use paging devices anymore because a new technology can fulfill a similar function more efficiently. Focusing on the tool at the expense of the purpose means that we shortchange our students.

We risk failing to prepare our students to be 21st century learners who can adapt to new technology because they understand the collaborative, cooperative, and communicative purposes that underlie the tool. As architect Frank Lloyd Wright noted, "Form follows function." When we keep the function in mind, the forms simply become part of our teaching repertoire.

Our list of functions and some current tools associated with them can be found in table I.1 (page 8). It's hard to write this knowing that by the time the book is printed, the tools will most likely have changed. Think of the list, then, as a historical reminder, and feel free to add new tools for the functions on the list as you discover them. Hopefully, the acknowledgment that tools change yet functions remain will reduce your stress a bit and allow you to select new tools for your teaching that will engage learners. Increasingly these tools are moving away from an emphasis on the device and toward sustained attention on the purpose.

Without question, the prudent use of such tools is an ongoing challenge. It seems like new technologies are greeted with suspicion at schools. We are not questioning the good intentions of those whose job it is to ensure a safe environment for students. But we do know that our profession has a long tradition of viewing any innovation as a negative—at one time, even chalkboards were thought to be a frivolous expense. From our vantage points as educational researchers and practitioners (Doug and Nancy) and technology coordinator (Alex), we have seen that when we foreground the function, conversations about common sense and good judgment about a particular tool become more logical.

What You Can Expect From This Book

This book is about the intersection of literacy and technology, and the ways in which each is shaping and informing the other. Given the short shelf life of technological tools, we know it is not wise to focus on "the latest and greatest" gadget. Instead, our discussion will follow the course we have mapped out in this introduction: keeping literacy in mind as we examine innovative applications of timeless functions. Our illustrations will mention particular tools, but please don't get caught up in the feasibility of adopting these tools at your school or in your district while looking past the functions.

We'll begin with a chapter on designing instruction to support the learning of 21st century skills in a literacy 2.0 environment. We think it's important to lay the groundwork for sound instruction and assessment here, since it informs the subsequent chapters. As part of this discussion, we will highlight the role that *purpose* plays in student learning. To foreshadow, purpose drives literacy 2.0: students ask "why" and then find, use, produce, and share information.

Table I.1: Technology Functions With Current Tools

Searching	Listening and Viewing	Storing
Google	podcasts	MP3 players
Yahoo	iTunes	flash drives
Lycos	screencasts	servers
Bing	Hulu	CDs/DVDs
phone apps	RSS feeds	e-books
StumbleUpon	streaming media	
Communicating	**Sharing**	**Collaborating**
Text messaging	YouTube	wikis
Twitter	blogs	VoiceThread
Digg	vlogs	Google Docs
video conferencing	Flickr	crowdsourcing
email	Picasa	
Producing	**Presenting**	**Networking**
GarageBand	PowerPoint	MySpace
iMovie	Keynote	Facebook
Comic Life	Wimba	Ning
Voki	smartboards	

Chapters 2 through 5 constitute the heart of the book, as they address many of the functions of literacy 2.0. In chapter 2, we examine what students need to learn about searching for information, particularly in digital environments. Information searches require students to use their literacy 1.0 skills, including decoding, word solving, vocabulary knowledge, and comprehension. However, many students improperly interpret and use the information they locate. Therefore, chapter 3 is dedicated to what students need to be taught about using information responsibly and, especially, avoiding plagiarism. This leads to chapter 4, a discussion of how students produce information, particularly in the context of new literacies. A significant aspect of new literacies is the shift in audience from the teacher alone to wider groups. Therefore, in chapter 5 we explore the implications of sharing information on local and global platforms.

Given the breathtaking changes occurring in literacy, technology, and education, in our final chapter we address some of the current challenges to school policies and practices and make a few predictions about the future of teaching and learning. In addition, we discuss the realities of classrooms that were built for 19th and 20th century literacy and the challenges of teaching in those physical environments in the 21st century. We also look at the policy environment that needs to change to fully realize the potential of literacy 2.0. Therefore, our conversation will return time and again to the ways in which we can equip our students with the skills and judgment they need to use technology in our schools and beyond.

Chapter Tweets

In keeping with our topic of literacy 2.0 within the 21st century, we will end each chapter with a series of microblog summary statements, all in 140 characters or less. Sometimes called "tweets," we like to think of them as 21st century haiku:

Wells' time traveler would not feel too out of place in today's classroom.

Don't throw out the literacy part of 21st century literacy. That's just foolish.

Form should always follow function. Thanks, Mr. Wright!

Chapter 1

Releasing Responsibility: A Framework for Teaching and Learning

Moving from a 20th century goal of student compliance to a 21st century goal of student competence requires an instructional model designed to accomplish this. The thinking behind the *gradual release of responsibility* model is that teachers must plan to move from providing students extensive support to having them rely on peer support to expecting them to function with no support. Or as Duke and Pearson (2002) suggested, teachers have to move from assuming "all the responsibility for performing a task . . . to a situation in which the students assume all of the responsibility" (p. 211). Unfortunately, in too many classrooms, releasing responsibility is unplanned, it happens too suddenly, and it results in misunderstandings and failure. Consider the classroom in which students hear a lecture and are then expected to pass a test. Or the classroom in which students are told to read texts at home and come to class prepared to discuss them. Or the classroom in which students are assigned a problem set twenty minutes after the teacher has explained how to do the problems. In each of these cases, students are expected to perform independently but are not well prepared for the task.

A Framework for the Gradual Release of Responsibility

Our interpretation of the gradual release of responsibility model includes four components: focus lessons, guided instruction, productive group work, and independent learning (Fisher & Frey, 2008a). The work we've done since 2001 suggests that implementing this instructional framework leads to significant improvement in student engagement and achievement. Having said that, we also want to emphasize that this is not a linear process and that teachers can implement the components in ways that are effective for their outcomes. Our criterion, however, for proper implementation of the framework is that all four components be present each time students and teachers meet. Let's explore each one.

Focus Lessons

A typical focus lesson lasts between ten and fifteen minutes. It is designed to do two things: establish a purpose and provide students with a model. The teacher often writes the purpose on the board and briefly discusses it with the students. Some teachers require that students include the purpose in their notes. Others make a verbal reference to the purpose several times during the class meeting. We aren't too concerned about where and how the purpose is listed; the important thing is that the students know what is expected of them and why they're learning what they're learning.

The second part of the focus lesson is the model. While volumes could be and have been written on modeling, middle and high school teachers rarely use this technique. Instead, they tend to provide procedural explanations that emphasize the *how* but not the *why*. Modeling, on the other hand, is metacognitive and includes the thinking behind the thinking. When students get a glimpse inside the thinking of an expert, they begin to approximate that behavior. Imagine the science student who gets to hear her teacher's understanding of an atom or the history student who witnesses the internal debate his history teacher has about sources of information. The models we provide students allow them access to academic language and thinking as well as information about expert problem solving and understanding. Daily modeling is critical if students are going to understand complex content.

In the literacy 2.0 classroom, modeling occurs in real time and is also augmented by the use of digital resources. For instance, a teacher can use Howcast videos to show demonstrations of throwing pottery on a potter's wheel, performing a Cruyff turn in soccer, or solving inequalities in algebra (www .howcast.com). Incorporating these resources enhances student access to the modeling, since the demonstrations can be viewed outside of the classroom. In addition, students are able to watch the demonstrations any number of times, allowing them to analyze specific aspects in order to answer their own questions.

Guided Instruction

Giving students a purpose and a model is not enough to ensure enduring understanding. Learners also need to be guided in their thinking. We define *guided instruction* as the strategic use of cues, prompts, and questions to get the student to do some of the cognitive work. The latter part of the definition is critical—guided instruction is intended to result in greater student understanding and is not simply a restatement of the information provided during a focus lesson. Guided instructional events, whether with the whole class or with small groups of students, are planned strategically so that teachers can understand student thinking and provide a precise scaffold.

We know that breakthrough learning occurs when teachers increase precision. Unfortunately, as Fullan, Hill, and Crévola (2006) point out, prescriptive teaching and not precision teaching is taking hold in our classrooms. Because students are not achieving, teachers are being provided with scripts to follow. Too often, these scripts do not allow for a gradual release of responsibility, as they cannot account for the vast range of individual differences and needs found in today's classroom.

A challenge to providing guided instruction in a busy classroom is that the teacher is limited in his or her ability to respond quickly to provide the necessary scaffold. However, technology can assist in minimizing this time gap. For example, a teacher can use his cell phone to send a text message that reads, "Confused? Reread 2nd paragraph, pg 82. I'll be right there." This allows the teacher to acknowledge the student's difficulty and give a cue to scaffold the student's understanding. The cue may or may not be sufficient, but the teacher will know this when he arrives at the student's side a few minutes later.

Productive Group Work

In order to learn, to really learn, students must be engaged in productive group tasks that require interaction. There are two keys to making this collaborative component effective. First, the tasks must give students the opportunity to use the language and content of the discipline with their peers. And second, students must be accountable for their individual contributions to the group so that the teacher knows which students understand the content and which ones need additional instruction. Together, these two factors increase engagement and provide teachers with formative assessment information that is useful in planning future instruction. These are also essential features of problem-based learning and project-based learning, which will be discussed later in this chapter.

This collaborative phase is at the heart of literacy 2.0, as evidenced by the changes we've seen since the late 20th century with regard to the manner in which students work together. Nearly all schools host a wiki for students to trade documents and work in a virtual environment. This tool is doing more than increasing convenience—it is changing the ways students are learning from one another. As members of a group write and edit a joint document, they are better able to respond to and build on one another's ideas. This is a much different process from one in which students work in isolation, coming together only to assemble the final product. Instead, it is possible for them to influence one another's understanding in real time, even when they are not in the same room.

Independent Learning

As part of instruction, students have to apply what they have been taught. Ideally, this step occurs under the guidance of the teacher as part of class time before homework is ever assigned. There are a number of in-class independent tasks that can help students master the content. For example, quickwrites allow students to clarify their thinking on a subject. They also provide teachers a glimpse into student understanding. Out-of-class independent learning—homework—should be saved until students have a firm grasp of the content. Simply said, students need practice before being asked to complete tasks entirely on their own. But in many classrooms, students are assigned tasks for homework without having been taught how to approach them. In response to a MetLife survey on homework, secondary teachers confessed that they "very often or often" assigned homework because they ran out of time in class (Markow, Kim, & Liebman, 2007, p. 30). The practice of assigning homework for missed class content will not result in student understanding. In fact, it is more likely to reinforce misunderstanding because in many cases students are practicing ineffectively and incorrectly. We will discuss homework and its relation to the gradual release of responsibility model in more detail in a later section of this chapter.

While homework may not be the best way for students to increase their understanding, digital tools are helping them to do so. For example, a student who creates and posts a podcast in which she describes the Battle of Britain for a radio audience develops and demonstrates not only mastery of the historical content but also a nuanced understanding of the medium and its effect on a population who could only hear, but not see, what was happening. Or a student who has stalled on his homework assignment can use dweeber.com, a social networking site for student collaboration. Dweeber (http://dweeber .com) allows students to solve problems together, participate in virtual study sessions, and communicate with others about schoolwork. Dweeber's "guiding principles" are ones that we can all learn from, as they are exceptionally consistent with learning in the 21st century:

- Everyone has their own unique brilliance.
- Think of differences as resources rather than disorders.
- Track assets rather than deficits.
- Think of mistakes as experiments rather than failures.
- Everyone has an inner Dweeb, a geek part of us that is passionate about something important. (Dweeber, 2009. Used with permission.)

Quality Indicators of the Gradual Release of Responsibility Framework

Now that we have described the four components of the gradual release of responsibility model, we can construct a picture of a classroom in which the framework is being effectively implemented. Table 1.1 lists the indicators that should be present for each component.

Table 1.1: Quality Indicators of the Gradual Release of Responsibility Model

Focus Lessons
The teacher establishes the purpose for the lesson.
The teacher uses "I" statements to model thinking.
The teacher uses questioning to scaffold instruction, not to interrogate students.
The lesson includes a decision frame for when to use the skill or strategy.
The lesson builds metacognitive awareness, especially of indicators of success.
Focus lessons move to guided instruction, not immediately to independent learning.
Guided Instruction
The teacher uses small-group arrangements.
Grouping changes throughout the semester.
The teacher has an active role in guided instruction; he or she does not just circulate and assist individual students.
There is a dialogue between learners and the teacher as they begin to apply the skill or strategy.
The teacher uses cues and prompts to scaffold understanding when a student makes an error, and he or she does not immediately tell the student the correct answer.
Productive Group Work
The teacher uses small-group arrangements.
Grouping changes throughout the semester.
The teacher has modeled the concepts students need to understand to complete collaborative tasks.

continued →

Productive Group Work
Students have received guided instruction in the concepts they need to understand to complete collaborative tasks.
Students are individually accountable for their contributions to the group.
The task provides students with an opportunity for interaction.
The task is a novel application of a concept or skill (not an exact duplication of what the teacher has modeled).

Independent Learning
Students have received modeled, guided, and collaborative learning experiences related to the concepts they need to understand to complete independent tasks.
Independent tasks extend beyond practice to application and extension of new knowledge.
The teacher meets with individual students for conferencing about the independent learning tasks.

Source: Better Learning Through Structured Teaching: A Framework for the Gradual Release of Responsibility, *by Douglas Fisher and Nancy Frey, pp. 127–129. Alexandria, VA: ASCD. © 2008 by ASCD. Adapted with permission. Learn more about ASCD at www .ascd.org.*

An instructional framework is one element in learning, but it must be coupled with interest, which is directly linked to motivation. It is sometimes incorrectly assumed that the only way to gain and hold a student's interest is to co-opt youth culture. We know from experience that this isn't true and further believe that certain themes have been sustained throughout human history precisely because they are so compelling. Perhaps the device that best propels students through learning is a single word: *why*. With more access to information than ever before, teachers need to compel their students to ask why and then show them how to answer this question.

Establishing Purpose: Always Asking Why

Anyone who has spent time with an adolescent recognizes the look: sweat-shirt hood pulled up, slack-jawed stare, head held slightly to one side like Nipper the dog in the old RCA advertisement. Next comes the inevitable question, in a voice somewhere between contempt and true puzzlement: "When am I ever going to need this?" Or there may be a subtler clue. A student who has learned to mask her bewilderment at the pointlessness of the lesson asks, "Is this going to be on the test?"

As educators, we love our content. We are moved by the delicacy of Shakespeare's sonnets or amazed at the orderliness that lies in fractals. Undoubtedly, we have spent years in and out of classrooms pursuing our interests in order to answer the questions that rivet us: How did the geography of New Orleans magnify the damage caused by Hurricane Katrina and the subsequent levee breaks? How are statistics being used to analyze the data gathered from Facebook quizzes? How do the Cirque du Soleil acrobats move so effortlessly? Our curiosity and content knowledge converge, and before we know it, we're searching for information to answer our own questions. It's unlikely that we pause at some point to ask ourselves about the purpose—it just *is*. And yet, for many of our students, there seems to be no point in learning about the interaction of geography and climate, or determining significance in statistics, or doing exercises that improve upper body flexibility.

One of the distinguishing aspects of 21st century learners is their search for purpose. We aren't suggesting that the generations of learners before them were merely sheep who needed only to follow. We craved purpose as well. But members of this generation are more vocal in their demand for it. They routinely seek relevance in tasks that capture their attention, and this applies to their reading and writing. As teachers, we need to understand the ways in which purpose and audience interface and plan lessons to develop students' understanding of both.

If you doubt the power of purpose, we invite you to read the following excerpt and pay particular attention to the information it presents about a house. As you read, consider the author's main idea. Really, pause here and take a look at this text:

> The two boys ran until they came to the driveway. "See, I told you today was good for skipping school," said Mark. "Mom is never home on Thursday," he added. Tall hedges hid the house from the road so the pair strolled across the finely landscaped yard. "I never knew your place was so big," said Pete. "Yeah, but it's nicer now than it used to be since Dad had the new stone siding put on and added the fireplace."
>
> There were front and back doors and a side door which led to the garage which was empty except for three parked 10-speed bikes. They went in the side door, Mark explaining that it was always open in case his younger sisters got home earlier than their mother.
>
> Pete wanted to see the house so Mark started with the living room. It, like the rest of the downstairs, was newly painted. Mark turned on the stereo, the noise of which worried Pete. "Don't worry, the nearest house is a quarter of a mile away," Mark shouted. Pete felt more comfortable observing that no houses could be seen in any direction beyond the huge yard.
>
> The dining room, with all the china, silver and cut glass, was no place to play so the boys moved into the kitchen where they made sandwiches.

> Mark said they wouldn't go to the basement because it had been damp and musty ever since the new plumbing had been installed.
>
> "This is where my Dad keeps his famous paintings and his coin collection," Mark said as they peered into the den. Mark bragged that he could get spending money whenever he needed it since he'd discovered that his Dad kept a lot in the desk drawer.
>
> There were three upstairs bedrooms. Mark showed Pete his mother's closet which was filled with furs and the locked box which held her jewels. His sisters' room was uninteresting except for the color TV which Mark carried to his room. Mark bragged that the bathroom in the hall was his since one had been added to his sisters' room for their use. The big highlight in his room, though, was a leak in the ceiling where the old roof had finally rotted. (Pichert & Anderson, 1977, p. 310)

That was probably a frustrating experience. Now, reread the information about the house with a different purpose. If your last name starts with a letter between A and M, read with the purpose of a homebuyer. If your last name starts with a letter between N and Z, read with the purpose of a burglar. A clearly defined purpose makes all the difference in the world, right? And that's what the study in which the house text was originally used suggested (Pichert & Anderson, 1977). When readers have a clear purpose, they perform better. Given that this study dates back to 1977, it's fair to say that purpose has been an important consideration in instruction for several decades. But today, learners demand purpose, in large part because of the number of things that compete for their attention.

Curricular design has undergone a revolution since the 1990s as educators have sought to make content more relevant to learners. In particular, we've witnessed a growing appreciation for using literacy 1.0 in service of other things, especially literacy 2.0 tasks such as finding, using, producing, and sharing information. The compartmentalizing of subject areas so prevalent in middle and high school conspires against learners, who quickly acclimate to the idea that biological knowledge only belongs in biology class, while mathematical thinking is only needed from 1:20 p.m. to 3:00 p.m. each day because that's when we have algebra. Algebra and biology teachers would be quick to note the connections—for example, algebraic thinking is necessary to understand how scientists measure loss of a species. Biology, the study of life systems, reinforces a learner's understanding of how Punnett squares are calculated to predict the outcomes of a breeding experiment.

What are needed are curricular approaches that encourage students to think across knowledge bases to build a schema of understanding. We must encourage our students to deploy all pertinent knowledge to solve interesting problems and projects. Cross-curricular thinking furthers the establishment of purpose and relevance in a literacy 2.0 world. Approaches that span subjects include problem-based learning and project-based learning. Although these methods are products of previous decades, they take on new meaning in the 21st century, as learners search for purpose and are systematically guided to a deeper understanding and an application of their knowledge.

Problem-Based Learning

Remember that one word, *why?* It is a human inclination to solve an interesting problem. That is the central premise behind problem-based learning (PBL). This curricular approach was pioneered in the medical field, where students are required to learn a large amount of information in a short period of time. Memorization alone is a poor substitute for the kind of learning that requires decision making, and so students at McMaster University were given cases in order to apply what they were learning. As Barrows and Tamblyn (1980) explained, "By working with an unknown problem, the student is forced to develop problem-solving, diagnostic, or clinical reasoning skills. He must get information, look for clues, analyze and synthesize the data available, develop hypotheses, and apply strong deductive reasoning to the problem at hand. This approach is very motivating to students" (p. 13).

Does this description of PBL sound like your job? Precisely. The intent of PBL is to create authentic situations that foster applying, analyzing, evaluating, and creating—those elusive critical-thinking skills first described by Benjamin Bloom in 1956 and then updated by Anderson and Krathwohl in 2001 to reflect the kinds of learning we think about today (see fig. 1.1). We can't help but notice that, in the updated taxonomy, Bloom's nouns have been changed to verbs.

Bloom's Taxonomy in 1956	has become . . .	Bloom's Taxonomy in the 21st Century
Evaluation		Creating
Synthesis		Evaluating
Analysis		Analyzing
Application		Applying
Comprehension		Understanding
Knowledge		Remembering

Figure 1.1: Bloom's taxonomy in the 21st century.

Problem-based learning units are sometimes organized by essential questions. These are thought-provoking questions that cannot be easily answered and are meant to encourage thinking across disciplines. This kind of consolidated thinking is necessary for building expertise and making decisions about complex issues. For example, an essential question that asks, "How do we affect our environment?" can foster thinking that includes knowledge about the biological and social sciences, fine and applied arts, service learning, and engineering. Essential questions that are used schoolwide can promote discussion across both disciplines and grade levels.

The updated Bloom's taxonomy is a useful tool for developing projects and assignments to explore essential questions. We align the assignments with the taxonomy to ensure that we are asking not merely a provocative question, but one that can result in authentic learning that is grounded in content standards. One schoolwide question we have used is "How do interactions affect your life?" We map out possible assignments related to this question that can invigorate classroom debate while advancing learning. Table 1.2 illustrates the kinds of assignments that high school students completed during a nine-week term, one of which was a direct response to the essential question itself. Of course, because we used the gradual release of responsibility model as our instructional framework, students also experienced teacher modeling and guided instruction while working productively with their peers on these assignments.

Students need to be informed about the world if they are to respond thoughtfully to essential questions. WebQuests, developed by Bernie Dodge (1995), are curricular units designed to build background knowledge while inviting students to explore a topic. Think of them as guided inquiry on the Internet. The teacher poses a question and identifies Web-based experiences that "focus on using information rather than looking for it" (Chandler, 2003, p. 38). Many WebQuests are designed so that the student progresses through formative lessons that lead to a culminating response to the question. Creating a WebQuest might seem simple, but in reality, it is much more complex than it might appear. T. J. Kopcha (2008), a colleague of Dodge's, created a series of short videos on developing WebQuests that are posted on YouTube.

A WebQuest is not meant to serve merely as a digital version of a textbook scavenger hunt. The collaborative and interactive aspects of a WebQuest, especially in the creation of new products or information, are critical. Since 1996, Dodge and his colleagues have been collecting WebQuests developed by teachers all over the world. The searchable database, now consisting of 2,500 units from grades K–12, is housed at www.webquest.org. Topics are as diverse as logarithms, the migration of the right whale, and Harriet Tubman. Many WebQuest assignments include grading rubrics and role tasks to encourage collaborative learning. In addition, they highlight the role that the teacher can take in providing instructional scaffolds, including modeling and guided instruction, so that students become successful.

Table 1.2: Using the Updated Bloom's Taxonomy to Explore an Essential Question

Bloom's Taxonomy	How do interactions affect your life?	Course
Creating	Develop an iMovie response to the essential question and post it on the school's wiki. View at least ten responses from your peers and write responses on the discussion board.	Schoolwide
Evaluating	What actions do you believe the U.S. government should have taken to limit the rise of totalitarian regimes in the post–World War I era?	World history
Analyzing	Analyze the interaction between positive and negative space in Picasso's *Les Demoiselles d'Avignon* (1907).	2-D visual arts
Applying	Write a proof for the Midpoint Theorem ("The coordinates of the midpoint of a line segment are the average of the coordinates of its endpoints").	Geometry
Understanding	Describe the interaction between setting, plot, and character in the novel you are reading.	English
Remembering	Create vocabulary cards for covalent and ionic bonds for the formation of large biological molecules.	Chemistry

The essential questions designed to fuel a problem-based learning unit or a WebQuest can be motivating to students, especially in establishing the purpose of learning about a particular topic. Project-based learning, a closely related curriculum design approach, can also be motivating for students.

Project-Based Learning

Though closely related to problem-based learning, project-based learning differs in its outcome. As noted in the previous section, the intent of problem-based learning is to create a purpose for learning by posing a problem that is not easily solved. The culminating student responses differ from one another quite a bit, as they are usually based in part on informed opinion. Project-based learning, on the other hand, focuses on the outcome itself. Students in a project-based learning unit are focused on creating a product. Another aspect of project-based learning is that it often provides a service to the community. An example of such a project from outside of education is the Eagle Scout leadership project of the Boy Scouts of America, which requires that the local community be the beneficiary.

Many school project-based learning assignments result in products that can be viewed or used by people outside of the classroom. High Tech High, a well-respected charter school in San Diego, has devoted a major portion of its curriculum to project-based learning. Middle and high school students produce a magazine focused on social issues, build and then teach about robotics to younger students in partner schools, create exhibits for the San Diego Maritime Museum, and make original short films for submission to local festivals. Examples of these and other projects can be viewed at www.hightechhigh.org/pbl/introduction.html. (Visit go.solution-tree.com/literacy for live links to the sites mentioned in this book.)

Project-based learning assignments are also useful for independent or contract learning. Todd, an eleventh-grade student at our school, had a deep level of knowledge and interest in the field of botany. He worked with a science professor from the local university on a yearlong project to design and care for plantings of native species for the outside of the school. The professor used WebQuests to build background knowledge, such as one focused on the use of native plants by Aboriginal people in Australia at http://science.uniserve.edu.au/school/quests/nativeplants.html. Over the course of the school year, Todd proposed species that would thrive in different areas, designed irrigation for the plants that would occupy the large cement pots near the parking lot, and tended the plants to propagate new growth. Along the way, Todd made mistakes, and his various teachers modeled for him and guided his learning, always with the project (outcome) in mind.

Project-based learning can be used to highlight classroom products as well. Tenth-grade world history teacher Simon Valerio teamed with the studio arts and English teachers to develop an exhibition called "Art, Life, and Death in the Great War." Students worked in teams to create a multimedia experience that included film, art, poetry, and informational displays. One group was assigned the task of designing and producing a display on trench art—the artifacts, such as jewelry and decorative objects, made by soldiers during World War I using found materials (usually military related). The students learned that, despite the genre's name, not all of the items were made in the trenches. In particular, some items were made by recuperating soldiers in convalescent hospitals. Others were made by prisoners of war. The students assembled digital photos of such pieces. Then they built an interactive work area in which they gathered present-day common classroom items (pencils, paper, rubber bands, and such) and asked visitors to make objects using these materials. Mr. Valerio contributed a few items that had been left behind in his classroom, including a carefully folded, masted boat made entirely out of chewing gum wrappers. "I guess this is life in our trenches," he chuckled.

Another group researched the poetry of the era and created digital shorts using various texts. For example, in one production, the lines of a well-known poem, "In Flanders Fields," by John McCrae, were accompanied by hip-hop performer Matisyahu's song "One Day." Still photographs of scenes of military cemeteries from all over the world slowly faded in and out. Denisha spoke about the origin of the poem, and her words were displayed on the screen: "The poem was sad, but I understood it more when I found out it was written by a surgeon in the Canadian Army who had just buried a young soldier he couldn't save."

In Flanders Fields

In Flanders fields the poppies blow
Between the crosses, row on row,
That mark our place; and in the sky
The larks, still bravely singing, fly
Scarce heard amid the guns below.

We are the Dead. Short days ago
We lived, felt dawn, saw sunset glow,
Loved, and were loved, and now we lie
In Flanders fields.

Take up our quarrel with the foe:
To you from failing hands we throw
The torch; be yours to hold it high.
If ye break faith with us who die
We shall not sleep, though poppies grow
In Flanders fields.

Project-based learning engages students by giving them authentic purposes for acquiring and analyzing information. In some cases, it also accomplishes the goal of moving learning closer to the local and global communities. Another curricular approach for community-based learning occurs in experiential educational experiences. New technologies make it possible to engage in experiences inside and outside classroom walls.

A true advantage of some of these technologies is that they have made it easier for students to continue their learning outside of the immediate company of the teacher. Of course, one particular type of learning is expressly designed to happen after the school day is over—homework. In the next section, we will discuss how homework can and should be a part of the gradual release of responsibility and how homework policies can be influenced by an understanding of literacy 2.0.

A New View of Homework

For all the changes that have occurred in instructional design, homework has remained rigidly consistent. This may be due in part to the expectations that families hold about homework. We have sometimes joked that everyone is an expert in school because everyone has been to third grade. Homework is the perfect case in point. Parents' beliefs about homework are often colored by their own personal experiences. If they had homework in third grade, then by all means their son or daughter should, too. The informal parent network is busy, as well. Parents call one another asking, "How much homework does your son have every night?" Homework is often viewed as a sign of rigor and high expectations. However, each family possesses its own algorithm for determining what is too much or not enough. Many families can share homework heartbreak stories about weeping children, missed dinners, and raised voices.

As mentioned earlier, we believe that a gradual release of responsibility model of instruction has a direct bearing on homework. When independent tasks are introduced too soon in the instructional cycle, it has a negative impact on students' interest and motivation. Where else but in a school would we expect to learn something for the first time and then replicate it without any further support or guidance eight or ten hours later? Yet in many classrooms, concepts are introduced in the morning and then students are expected to apply them, alone, in homework assignments that evening. What if, instead, homework were used to build fluency, apply previously learned skills, review older material, and extend previously learned skills?

Fluency Building

Rapid retrieval of information is a hallmark of learning. Whether students are reading, working on mathematical problems, or writing a paper, they must be able to retrieve related information fluidly in order to concentrate on the matters at hand. Readers need a strong foundation in the alphabet of the language, while math students need to know their math facts. Writers need to be able to write or type quickly. Without fluency in these basic skills, the complexities of reading, math, and writing will elude the learner. Homework that focuses on building fluency allows students to practice using familiar skills and concepts. Fluency-building assignments may include flashcards, online games, or timed reading and writing tasks. Students engaged in fluency-building homework compete with themselves to improve their time or rate. There are many software programs designed to provide practice to increase fluency in math skills, reading, and writing. As one teacher told us, "The advantage of these programs is that they never wear out, lose patience, or get bored." A typing tutor is a simple example, and it is a tool that not only helps students become more proficient in using a keyboard but also teaches them to read the information on screen and process it as they type. This input-process-output sequence engages the students with both the information and the mechanical process.

Application

Application is a step beyond fluency. At this level, students are applying what they know to new situations. The practice of assigning a specific number of minutes of reading each night is an ideal example of giving homework that emphasizes application. Some of our colleagues assign podcasts or Internet-based videos for homework. In some cases students are asked to listen to a specific podcast or watch a specific video and in other cases they're asked to create podcasts or videos. These assignments are intended to provide students with time to utilize concepts that are becoming more familiar to them in a context that is new. An online-research or scavenger-hunt type of project can allow students the opportunity to exercise their knowledge of their surrounding technology to gain knowledge related to their assigned objective.

Spiral Review

This is the type of homework assignment we use most frequently in our practice. Rather than devote the six weeks before state tests to lots of cramming, we spread test preparation out across the year. Our homework assignments routinely consist of practice with concepts that were previously taught, either earlier in the same year or, in some cases, even one or two years before. This approach is especially helpful when students will be taking tests that are designed to measure cumulative instruction. For instance, the eighth-grade social studies test for California extends back to information taught in fifth grade. Rather than fret about how much students have retained, we give homework assignments designed to draw on content from previous grades. During the eighth-grade unit on American democracy, for example, the homework assignments focus on the democratic contributions of ancient Greece and Rome, a sixth-grade content standard. In this way, the homework becomes the vehicle for activating the background knowledge needed to master new content. An instructor could maintain a wiki and update it throughout the year, documenting the progression of the class content. This site would become a good source of review material for the students.

Extension

A final productive approach to homework is using it to challenge students to extend their learning beyond what they have learned in the classroom. Interest is vital here, and many of the homework assignments we give are negotiated individually with students in the form of a learning contract. Each semester, we ask students to extend their learning about a topic of their choice that is related to the course content. Shannon, a ninth-grader recently diagnosed with a math learning disability, chose to research mathematicians to gain insight into the background of the concepts she was learning. She found out about a group of UCLA mathematicians who won a $100,000 prize in 2008 for identifying a particular kind of prime number called a Mersenne Prime, which contains almost 13 million digits. Shannon was intrigued by this and learned about Mersenne, a French monk from the 16th century, and Alan Turing, the mathematician who revolutionized the search for these numbers in 1949 by using an electronic digital computer. She learned that Turing was a British citizen who worked on breaking the code for the Enigma machine, the encryption machine the Nazis used to send secret messages. Her initial interest in mastering integers led her first to number theory, then to the Mersenne Prime, and finally to a mathematician whose work contributed to the ending of the war in Europe. Although Shannon is still not a huge fan of algebra, her homework extension project led her to understand a purpose of the discipline. "I never understood why I had to know about numbers that didn't exist," she told us. "Now at least I have an idea about what someone can do with that kind of knowledge. And apparently, there's money in it!"

Table 1.3 summarizes the points that teachers should consider as they develop homework geared toward the four purposes we have just discussed.

Practices such as homework endure and should be shaped by the knowledge and skills to be expected of a 21st century citizen. Another practice fundamental to teaching is gathering assessment data for the purpose of informing instruction. Indeed, the output of students using a variety of tools increases the pressure on teachers to collect, analyze, and respond to the learning patterns in evidence. This requires embedding assessment into instruction in order to maximize face-to-face interactions with students.

Table 1.3: Checklist for Developing Effective Homework Assignments

Purpose of Homework	Characteristics	Reflective Questions to Ask
Fluency building	Gives multiple opportunities for practice	Are there ways to ensure that students engage in the task multiple times?
	Focuses on one or two skills	Is the number of skills required limited so that students can build fluency?
	Serves as an access point for other skills or knowledge	Is the difficulty level low enough so that students can focus on speed/rate/fluency, instead of how the skill is performed?
Application	Allows a skill to be used to solve a problem or apply a rule or principle	What rule or principle will the students use to solve the problem?
	Uses previously learned skill for a new situation	Do the students possess the background knowledge and prior experiences necessary to understand the new or novel situation?
Spiral review	Allows students to utilize previously learned skills or knowledge	What previously taught skills or knowledge are important for future learning and assessment?
	Allows students to confirm their understanding and assess their own learning	In what ways will this strengthen students' metacognitive awareness of how well they use skills and knowledge?
	Relates conceptually to current learning	What previously taught skills or knowledge serve as a basis for current classroom instruction?
Extension	Has potential for development of new understandings	Does the assignment lead to a new knowledge base or set of concepts?
	Results in a new product or innovation	Will the students create a new product or innovation that they have not done before?
	Requires the use of a variety of skills or knowledge	What skills or knowledge will students need to complete the assignment?

Source: Fisher, D., & Frey, N. (2008b), p. 43. Used with permission.

Using Assessment for Instruction

Assessment *of* learning, or summative assessment, provides teachers and students with information about the attainment of content knowledge. Summative assessments often result in grades. In future chapters, we will present several ideas for using technology for summative assessment. For now, we'd like to focus on assessment *for* learning, or formative assessment, which is used to check students' understanding and to plan subsequent instruction. Teachers can check for understanding in a number of ways, including asking questions, giving writing assignments, assigning projects and performances, and giving tests (Fisher & Frey, 2007a). The information gained from formative assessments guides the next steps in instruction and helps teachers and students consider the additional learning opportunities needed to ensure success.

Formative assessment information must be fed forward into an instructional model that allows for responsiveness to student need—ideally, the gradual release of responsibility model (Fisher & Frey, 2009). If the formative assessment—such as a writing sample, a quiz, or a series of postings on a discussion board—suggests that significant numbers of students did not master the content, the teacher should design additional focus lessons to facilitate students' understanding. If several students make the same error, they probably need additional guided instruction from the teacher. If students are confusing information or not applying what they know to novel situations, they probably need more collaborative learning and independent learning opportunities.

Consider the following example of how Ms. Enriquez, an English teacher, assessed her students' understanding and then planned her instruction accordingly. The students in Ms. Enriquez' class were exploring the essential question "Does age matter?" They completed a number of tasks, including reading widely on the subject of age and creating their own websites to answer the question. The students were free to determine the contents of their websites but were required to include specific components based on the standards and what was taught. Adrianna wrote the following poem (used with permission) and posted it on her site:

Confidence

Thinking of me

Thinking of my life

Thinking of what I have done

Thinking of what I want

Will I be happy

Will I always hurt

Will I be confident

Will I always be unsure

When will I believe

More in me than them

When will I believe

that I am worthy

of it all

when will it

become part of me

when will my

confidence

never leave me

When Ms. Enriquez analyzed this poem, she noted Adrianna's success with the assignment. In fact, across the class, students performed very well on their poetry. Ms. Enriquez didn't feel the need to use any focus lesson time on this standard. She also noticed Adrianna's lack of punctuation. Given that the context was a poem and poets are allowed license, she wasn't too worried about that but decided to meet with Adrianna and three other students who had not used correct punctuation. While she gave this small group guided instruction focused on punctuation, the rest of the students would work collaboratively or independently on tasks that still needed to be completed.

Ms. Enriquez started the conversation with the group on a positive note:

Ms. Enriquez: Let me start by saying how wonderful I think your poems are. You really expressed yourselves. I bet you're really proud of your poetry.

Students: Thanks. Thank you. Good. Yeah.

Ms. Enriquez: I also know that, like other poets, you took some liberties in your writing. I think that this is wonderful. I think it's a brilliant move to play with the rules of language in poetry, which all of you did, just like the poets we studied.

Brian: Yeah, and I gotta break some rules!

Ms. Enriquez: So true. And as your English teacher, I just need to check and see that you know which rules you broke. You see, poets know which rule to break to get the effect they want. So take a minute and look at your poems again.

I printed them from your websites. Now don't edit, they're beautiful just the way they are. Instead, list the rule you broke as a poet, and show me evidence for the rule breakage. (The students look at their papers and begin reading and writing.)

Julio: See, here. I didn't capitalize so that it would make the word less important than it would be regular. See, here again. And this one.

Adrianna: I didn't use periods or commas so that my reader wouldn't know where to stop.

Ms. Enriquez: If you were writing this in a more conventional way, where might you add punctuation?

Adrianna: After almost every line. Like here (points) and here (points) but not here (points).

Ms. Enriquez: Perfect. Love it. So now I want all of you to do the same thing on your websites. Take a look at all of the pages you've created and check the punctuation. I noticed when I reviewed them that you have taken liberties with capitalization and punctuation. But I'm not sure your readers would give you the same license as when they read your poems. So go back and proofread your websites and see whether those differences are contributing to or detracting from your message. Then make the revisions you need. I'll be around to help you.

In this case, Ms. Enriquez had assessment information that suggested that her students might not understand common writing conventions. Given that she had no evidence that the entire class needed this content, she decided to meet with a small group rather than reteach the content to the class as a whole. She'll follow up with this group of students as they revise their websites and will have similar conversations with them about conventions and how poetic license does and does not apply in a virtual environment. This kind of individualized teaching is what the gradual release of responsibility framework allows. We presented the model at the beginning of this chapter as a planning tool, which is it. But equally important is the idea that the gradual release of responsibility model can be used to address issues that arise during formative assessments.

Chapter Tweets

Memory and learning are iterative and recursive. Each is dependent on the other.

Scaffolded learning builds toward mastery through focus lessons, guided instruction, productive group work, and independent learning.

Focus lessons are short and give the teacher an opportunity to model how a content expert applies his or her thinking in order to reach understanding.

Guided instruction is notable for the strategic use of cues, prompts, and questions to help the student do the cognitive work.

Collaborative learning with peers should result in productive group work, not the equal division of a task for later assembly.

Independent learning is the ultimate goal, as self-directed learning is a hallmark of 21st century learning.

Without purpose, learners struggle to retain information beyond the next test and often fail to take learning to the levels of analysis, evaluation, and creation.

Curricular design organized around an intriguing problem, project, or experience will establish purpose and increase relevance.

Homework can be useful when intentionally designed for fluency, application, spiral review, or extension.

Chapter 2

Finding Information: The Eternal Search

There is more information at our fingertips today than ever before. Remember doing a research project in high school? You had to physically go to the library and search the card catalog. Then you had to find the green books, *Guides to Periodicals*, to see where the journals you wanted were located (if your library had them). For example, Doug remembers an assignment from tenth grade related to World War I. The teacher wanted personal accounts of people who lived through the war, as well as factual information regarding the war. Doug went to the card catalog and looked up the subject "World War I." There were several entries, and Doug hunted each of them down. Some were useful for his paper, but most were not. Doug used an ineffective search strategy that consumed a lot of time.

Sound familiar? While the tools students use today to search for information have changed, the strategies they use have not. As their teachers, we have to instruct them in conducting effective information searches. This chapter will focus on efforts to help students locate information. But literacy 2.0 requires more than an effective search strategy. Unlike the sources Doug would have found from the card catalog, the Internet provides students with unfiltered information. Spurious screeds sit alongside valid information. Accordingly, we also have to teach students how to evaluate the information they find. The gatekeepers of information from the past no longer exert their control over what students find, and this presents additional challenges for the 21st century teacher.

Gatekeeping in Literacy 2.0

In the past, there were a number of gatekeepers that filtered information students would see. Materials were reviewed and approved. There were editors

and publishers and committees that sorted which information was "appropriate" for students and which was not. The Internet changed all of that. Just
about anyone can post just about anything for the public to find. In some
respects this system is a great thing, as ideas flow freely among and between
people. On the flip side, there are more opportunities for the public to be misled
or misinformed. Of course, the Internet did not create scam artists. Remember
the "quacks" at the turn of the century who traveled around the country with
their medicine that cured everything (www.collectmedicalantiques.com/quack
.html)? The difference today is the scale and reach of questionable claims.

Having said that, the Internet is remarkably accurate, especially given
the public nature of its contributions. It seems that the watchdogs are out in
force to counter the claims that do not have evidence. There are even websites
devoted to debunking the myths, and our favorite is www.snopes.com. As we
were writing this book, we visited Snopes to investigate a rumor that was cir-
culating at the time: "The CDC says swine flu is wiping out villages in Asia
and will kill 60 percent of the U.S. population." We'd heard this rumor from
several reliable sources, including a guest speaker who came to our school to
talk about the importance of infection prevention. While infection prevention
techniques are indeed important, we learned from Snopes that the rumor was
absolutely false, and the claim that 60 percent of the U.S. population would
die wasn't an accurate representation of the information from the Centers for
Disease Control.

Wikipedia is an interesting case to consider in the discussion of gatekeeping.
Written by anyone who wants to contribute, it has become the most frequently
used encyclopedic resource in the world. But many teachers forbid students
from using it, based on the perception that it's not very accurate because it
lacks quality controls and gatekeepers. But a study published in *Nature* (Giles,
2005) suggested that the entries in Wikipedia were only slightly less accurate
than those in *Britannica*. When *Britannica* disputed the claim, *Nature* clarified
the methodology, noting that the forty-two experts who carried out the review
did not know if they were reading an entry from Wikipedia or from *Britannica*
("Britannica Attacks," 2006).

To be honest, we often start our search for information with Wikipedia. It's
quick, reasonably accurate, and fairly comprehensive in terms of topics. And it
updates in real time, unlike the print encyclopedias sitting on our shelves that
we can't bear to recycle. It is also important to know that from time to time
Wikipedia will temporarily lock an entry if rapidly changing events are causing
lots of conflicting posts. For example, the entry for Bill Ayers was suspended for
a time during the presidential campaign of 2008 because of the number of postings that violated Wikipedia's requirements for neutrality and outside sources.
(Click on the Discussion tab of any Wikipedia entry to view the debates about

information in an entry, and use the History feature to view edits.) Naturally, it's not the only source we use, and we know how to use it based on the task at hand. We know, for example, the difference between using Wikipedia to find out something that interests us (like a search Nancy just did about Chuck Close photorealistic paintings) and using Wikipedia when writing research articles. And that's one of the things we have to teach our students.

Teaching With Wikipedia

There are a number of ways for teachers to harness the power of the 2,000,000 + entries in Wikipedia, the first of which is to use the resource during modeling. As you recall from chapter 1, teacher modeling is an important component of the gradual release of responsibility. Biology teacher James Franklin models various skills while reading Wikipedia entries aloud. During one lesson, for example, he projects the Wikipedia page about decomposers (en.wikipedia.org/wiki/Decomposer). Starting with the photograph of fungi on a tree, Mr. Franklin activates his background knowledge, makes predictions, figures out words from the context clues provided, and makes connections between the information on the Wikipedia page and the textbook the students use. As part of his modeling, he tells his students:

> *Decomposer* is an easy term for me to remember because I know that *compose* is to put things together and that the prefix *de-* is the opposite. That's how I remember the meaning of the decomposers, generally. But as they say here, there is more technical information about decomposers. I see the parentheses and the word *or,* so I know that they're providing me with another word for the same idea. *Saprotrophs* is another word for decomposer. But I'm going to click that word and see what else it tells me, because it shows up here in blue. That means it's hyperlinked. Here it tells me that in addition to decomposer and saprotroph, they're also called "detritus feeders." Now I have three names for these types of feeders.

Mr. Franklin continues working his way through the text, modeling his thinking as he goes. At the end of the entry, he notices the warning, which indicates that the page has references but no inline citations. He tells the class,

> Oh, this is a page that I have to be careful with. There are references, and the references are to professional articles and books, but there aren't citations in the text that suggest where each idea comes from. That doesn't mean the information isn't accurate, but rather that I should check with other sources before using the information. As a quick check, I think I'll take a peek at the textbook and read a few paragraphs to see if there are ideas that differ.

In using Wikipedia in this way, Mr. Franklin alerts his students to a few key ideas. First, he signals to the class that he knows about Wikipedia, which will help prevent plagiarism and the inappropriate use of content from this website. Second, he shows them that Wikipedia is a useful resource but one that has to be checked, like all other sources. And finally, he demonstrates how a purposeful user can utilize a Wikipedia entry to get an overview that can lead him or her to additional information.

Of course, modeling isn't the only use for Wikipedia in the classroom. Margaret Santori uses Wikipedia to build students' understanding of discussing ideas and to show them that disagreements can arise during these types of discussions. Using the Discussion tab on a given Wikipedia page, Ms. Santori invites students to analyze the ways in which people engage with one another. For example, there is a lengthy discussion on T. S. Eliot's page about his anti-Semitic views. Ms. Santori points out to her class that the individuals who contributed to the discussion did so in ways that were respectful of others. In one entry, the writer asks if Eliot's body of work "actually added to it [anti-Semitism] and nourished it." The conversation continues for several pages, with people adding their perspectives and references, all the while maintaining a respectful discussion. One person writes about Emanuel Litvinoff, a Jewish poet who, at a meeting with Eliot present, read a poem in which he "accused Eliot of, at best, indifference to the suffering of the Jews during WW2." Litvinoff's name is hyperlinked to another entry in Wikipedia that provides more information about him and his body of work, including a discussion of his human rights work.

As Ms. Santori notes, "This is the kind of discussion educated people have. It's civil, even when we disagree. And that's the kind of discussions we'll have in this class. You don't have to agree with one another about the topics and readings, but you do have to argue your position with evidence and compassion for others." In this case, Wikipedia has provided an example for behavior expected in the classroom.

These two examples of using Wikipedia in the classroom point to another important factor in literacy 2.0, which is becoming known as "three-dimensional reading."

Three-Dimensional Reading

We don't know who first coined the term *three-dimensional reading*, but we hear it all the time at conferences. In fact, it's becoming part of the educational lingo that teachers and researchers use to discuss Internet-based reading. In the old days of print-based reading, reading occurred in two dimensions: left to right and top to bottom. That's how you're reading this page. And two-dimensional reading applied to nearly everything we read, from novels to newspapers. While you could skip around, once you started reading something, you either read in the two-dimensional fashion or you abandoned your reading. In essence, the author was in control of the print and the way you experienced it.

But that no longer applies. Internet reading is three-dimensional. With hyperlinks, the reader is on a self-directed journey and may never finish the original page of information. With three-dimensional reading, we read across, down, and into. As blogger SayUncle says, "By hyperlinking something, the writer adds another place for you to go with respect to reading what they're trying to say. These links are usually facts, sometimes humor, or stuff that only serves to waste your time" (SayUncle, 2002).

As a case in point, we observed as a student used the Internet to find information about the Ring of Fire. To reduce some of the variability, we pointed her to a specific webpage to start with: http://geography.about.com/cs/earthquakes/a/ringoffire.htm. (More on teaching students to search for information is presented later in this chapter.)

The page begins with a definition and a hyperlinked map from the U.S. Geological Survey. Shelene doesn't choose that link but reads down the page a bit. She types, "75% of all volcanoes are in the ring of fire" into her note page and keeps reading. She comes to a sponsored link and selects it. This takes her to a YouTube video of Johnny Cash singing "Ring of Fire" in 1963. She lets it play for a minute or so, laughs, and returns to the primary page. At the bottom of the page, she selects "maps of the Ring of Fire" and takes a look, but not for long, as she returns to the primary page and chooses "worst disasters in the 20th century." There are hundreds of words on this page, not hyperlinked. Shelene scans down the page, apparently not reading anything, and finds a link to "2004 Deadliest Earthquake Year in Five Centuries." After reading a few paragraphs (with no hyperlinks), she scrolls to the bottom of the page and selects "New York City Earthquake." No longer in the Ring of Fire, but not knowing it, Shelene adds notes about this earthquake to her open page.

We could go on, but suffice it to say that Shelene was acquiring information but not necessarily the information that she needed for her Ring of Fire project. The three-dimensional text was no match for her two-dimensional skills. She needs—no, she deserves—to be taught to find information in a three-dimensional landscape.

Teaching Students to Find Information

If you were asked to find out something, say, the name of the twenty-second president of the United States, where would you go? How would you find the information? If you're like most of the world, you'd Google it. According to Alexa, a company that tracks Web traffic (www.alexa.com), Google is the most frequently visited site in the world. The top ten sites in the United States (as of this writing) are:

1. Google—www.google.com

2. Facebook—www.facebook.com

3. Yahoo!—www.yahoo.com

4. YouTube—www.youtube.com

5. MySpace—www.myspace.com

6. Amazon—www.amazon.com

7. Wikipedia—www.wikipedia.com

8. eBay—www.ebay.com

9. Windows Live—www.live.com

10. Blogger—www.blogger.com

Before we continue, let's take a minute and consider how the Web is most commonly used. Of the top ten sites, four are used for finding information, two for sharing information, two for connecting people, and two for online buying.

Most of us have used search engines to find information and know the basics of doing so. To search for the twenty-second president of the United States, most of us will go to Google and type "22nd president of the U.S." Using Google in this way provides easy access to accurate information. The first and second entries that will come up from this search will be from Wikipedia and will say that Grover Cleveland is the answer. As is the case with most Web searches, we will probably also learn something additional along the way. For example, we might not have remembered that Cleveland was the only president to serve two nonconsecutive terms or that his first name was Stephen.

But this search strategy isn't as efficient or effective when the topic is more general. When Corima selected the topic of women's roles in World War I, her initial Google search for **World War I** resulted in 143,000,000 webpages. Remember that this included pages that had the word *world* but not *war* or *I*. It also included pages that had the word *war* but not *world* or *I*. But Google is fairly sophisticated, and the first several pages of results that came up were about World War I, including the first entry, which was from Wikipedia.

How can we help this student narrow her search and find information specifically about the experience of women in World War I? Adding *women* to the search string (**World War I women**) results in more pages—153,000,000—not fewer. Corima needs to understand some simple commands to limit her search.

Boolean Operators

There are a number of Boolean search tools (www.internettutorials.net/boolean.asp) that Corima can quickly use to get more targeted results:

- Quotation marks—One of the ways we teach students to limit their searches is to place quotation marks around the search terms so that the pages found include the words in the exact string as written. For Corima, adding quotation marks around *World War I* and leaving *women* in the search string reduces the number of pages to 7,310,000. Of course, students can overuse the quotation marks. When Corima quoted her entire topic (**"World War I women's roles"**) she had only eight results, none of which were particularly helpful.

- + (plus sign)—This works similarly to the quotation marks used for phrases but is confined to single words. That is, it limits the search to pages that have all of the words, but the words do not have to appear in a particular sequence. One disadvantage of using this method is that most search engines automatically employ synonyms, so a person might end up with other terms that are not needed for a particular search.

- OR—Some terms are used interchangeably, and the person doing the search doesn't want to lose valuable information by limiting the search to only one term. For example, World War I is also known as the First World War. By adding OR between the two common names (both in quotation marks), Corima made her search more inclusive and ensured that the information returned would have one or the other of these two common terms. Of course, this increased the number of pages that Corima had to consider (25,000,000), but important information might have been omitted if she had not specified the interchangeable terms.

- AND—Another way for students to modify their search is with the term AND. This limits the search to pages with both of the terms, not just either one. When Corima typed **"World War I" OR "First World War" AND women AND role** (with "World War I" in quotes), the number of results she obtained was reduced to 7,970,000. The AND function provides additional guidance for the search engine and helps target appropriate pages for the user.

- NOT or — (minus sign)—When the person doing the search knows that there are a number of items that are commonly associated with the topic but that those items are not of interest, the modifier NOT is helpful. This removes the pages that have contents related to the exclusion criteria. In Corima's case, she was not interested in women pilots because her friend was writing about that topic. So her search string read: **"World War I" OR "First World War" AND women AND role NOT pilot** (with "World War I" in quotes). The result was 45,800 pages that were very likely to contain information she could use.

Advanced Search Operators

Students can also search for information using specific terms, called "advanced search operators" or "meta words," to narrow searches. This method is especially useful when one knows about the existence of information and needs to locate it again. These words are used to preface search terms and are followed by a colon and then the desired information. Note that there is no space after the colon.

- **Site:** limits information to the domain name. For example, a student who wants information about hurricanes would type in **site:noaa.gov/hurricanes** to narrow the search to the 28,500 websites within the noaa.gov domain.

- **Link:** narrows a search to links to a particular website. For instance, the entry **link:www.noaa.gov** shows the 15,000 websites that have linked to this url address.

- **Inurl:** refines the search to Web addresses that feature the key terms. Therefore, **inurl:hurricane** yields 1,750,000 webpages with the term *hurricane* in the url address.

- **Intitle:** further restricts a search by identifying terms in indexed titles. A search of **intitle:hurricane + noaa** locates 69,500 indexed titles (usually documents) that contain the words *hurricane* and *NOAA*.

Specialized Search Engines

In addition to learning how to use search terms, students also need to know that there are specialized search engines that can be used to locate specific types of information. We are especially interested in the Directory of Open Access Journals (www.doaj.org) and have had great success with students using this search tool when they need technical information. For example, Jared was looking for information about toxoplasmosis for his health seminar and internship. Using DOAJ, he found 140 articles in which this topic appeared. The second entry, from the *International Journal of Medical Sciences,* included treatment information for ocular toxoplasmosis, which was what Jared needed in his case report.

We also like Search Engine Showdown (www.searchengineshowdown.com/features), as it provides current information about the top search engines and how they compare with one another. We ask students to use this as their starting page so that they purposefully select a search engine that matches their need.

Necessary Skills

Of course, teaching about specialized search tools assumes that students know how to use a search engine. Unfortunately, there is evidence that some students simply type directly into the address bar and hope they find something useful. For example, a student might type www.worldwar1.com into the address bar. Had Corima done this, she would have been lucky and would have been directed to a site devoted to teaching about World War I. A student who types worldwar1.net gets a site for sale with no information.

To address this instructional need, Donald Leu and his colleagues (2008) developed a checklist of skills students should master related to Internet use. A few of the items on their Teaching Internet Comprehension to Adolescents assessment include the ability to:

- Locate at least one search engine.
- Use several of the following general search engine strategies during key word entry:
  - Topic and focus
  - Single and multiple key word entries
  - Phrases for key word entry
- Use several of the more specialized search engine strategies during key word entry:
  - Quotation marks
  - Paraphrases and synonyms
  - Boolean
  - Advanced search tool use
- Select from a variety of search engine strategies to locate useful resources when an initial search is unsuccessful:
  - Knows the use and meaning of the "Did you mean . . . ?" feature in Google.
  - Adjusts search engine key words according to the results of a search.
  - Narrows the search.
  - Expands the search.
  - Reads the search results to discover the correct vocabulary and then use this more appropriate vocabulary in a new search.
  - Shifts to another search engine. (Leu et al., 2008, pp. 343–44)

Teaching students how to search for information is only the first part of finding information. Once the search results are in, students have to determine if the information is useful and credible.

Teaching Students to Evaluate the Information They Find

With the number of hits most searches uncover, it's overwhelming to figure out which are useful and which are not. Everyone has gone on a journey through the Internet, starting with a search for one thing and finding something else entirely. While this serendipity is sometimes fun and can be very informative, students need to be able to find specific information that is credible.

We like to start each school year (and sometimes each new project) with general conversations with students about the fact that there is bogus information on the Web. Donald Leu showed us a bogus website designed for the fictitious Pacific Northwest Tree Octopus (http://zapatopi.net/treeoctopus) and reported that nearly all of the middle school students in a study he and his colleagues conducted believed that there was such a creature and that it was endangered (Krane, 2006). Given that we teach in California, we're partial to the information the Web offers about Velcro crops and their sustainability, so we often start class with a discussion of the website devoted to this matter (http://home.inreach.com/kumbach/velcro.html). Many of our students believe that the site contains "important and accurate information" and even argue with us after we announce that the information is fake. Like most adults, our students were raised on the phrase "You can't believe everything you read." But like us, they do anyway. In this respect, Internet credibility isn't new. For decades, teachers have worked to instill a healthy dose of skepticism in readers and to teach students to question what they read. That's no different today.

Our current efforts to address the reliability of Internet sources are based on the work of Robert Harris (2007), who developed the "CARS [Credibility, Accuracy, Reasonableness, Support] Checklist for Information Quality." Table 2.1 is his summary of the checklist.

We use this tool to help students focus on various aspects of a website as they make decisions about the usefulness of the page. For example, seventh-grade science student Sean was looking for information on solar energy. In limiting his search, he found the site www.facts-about-solar-energy.com. As he investigated the site, he considered its credibility, accuracy, reasonableness, and support. Sean thought that the site was credible because it gave contact information for the authors of the site. He was impressed that the site originated in Australia because, to his mind, people "wouldn't care so much about politics there," which he felt added to the site's credibility. He also thought the site was accurate because it presented both the pros and cons of solar energy and provided a lot of information for each topic that it addressed. But he noted that the site hadn't been updated since 2006, which caused him some concern.

As he said, "The ads on the website are more current than some of the info on it. Like, they have Obama's plan in the ads, but the cost isn't right anymore. So there might be other things that are not current." On a more positive note, Sean thought that the information was reasonable and objective, even though the creators of the site were clearly advocates for solar energy. And the support the site provided seemed fairly good, as it referred people to lots of "different resources and places to get solar, rather than trying to send people all to one place." While Sean might be somewhat naïve about the contents of any website, he does know what to look for and can fairly easily spot sites that are designed solely to sell something or to persuade readers. He is developing a habit of looking at websites with a more critical eye, and hopefully, by the time he completes his schooling, he will be a critical consumer of Web resources.

Table 2.1: Summary of the CARS Checklist for Research Source Evaluation

Credibility	Trustworthy source, author's credentials, evidence of quality control, known or respected authority, organizational support. Goal: an authoritative source, a source that supplies some good evidence that allows you to trust it.
Accuracy	Up-to-date, factual, detailed, exact, comprehensive, audience and purpose reflect intentions of completeness and accuracy. Goal: a source that is correct today (not yesterday), a source that gives the whole truth.
Reasonableness	Fair, balanced, objective, reasoned, no conflict of interest, absence of fallacies or slanted tone. Goal: a source that engages the subject thoughtfully and reasonably, concerned with the truth.
Support	Listed sources, contact information, available corroboration, claims supported, documentation supplied. Goal: a source that provides convincing evidence for the claims made, a source you can triangulate (find at least two other sources that support it).

Source: Harris, R. (2007). Reprinted by permission.

Sometimes students have difficulty mastering the general concepts Harris outlined. In these cases, we formalize their review of websites using an evaluation tool like the one in figure 2.1 (page 44). When students use this tool, we meet with them to discuss what they found and to talk them through their analysis. Over time, we can reduce their use of this formal tool and return them to the general criteria.

In addition to teaching students how to find and evaluate information, we can teach them how to use information that has been collected and assembled by others. The new website-sharing tools can help students find more information than ever before when they know how to use them.

URL: _____

1. Title of website: _____

2. What is the main purpose of the website? (Is it selling something? Does it describe a service? Is it an educational site?)

   _____

3. Who created the website? (Is there a contact name? Is it a private company? Is it a school? Is it a government agency? Is there an "about us" section?) _____

4. How current is the website? (When was it last updated?)

   _____

5. Are links available to other sites? (Try some of them to make sure they work.)

   _____

6. Are there references or citations? _____ If yes, what are they?

   _____

7. What new information did you learn from this website?

   _____

   _____

8. What information is missing?

   _____

   _____

Figure 2.1: Website evaluation tool.

Social Bookmarking

Just as we might use a sticky note or fold the corner of a page in a book to know where we left off, we can *bookmark* website links (or add them to our *favorites* list) for future reference. All Web browsers offer this feature. The bookmarked data are stored in the computer user's Web browser profile. This profile is a folder or file that contains all of the preferences and configurations set by the user. The role of the profile is to remember what the user likes and how he or she wants the browser to present, remember, and process information on the Web. Though bookmarking is a very useful feature to help store and categorize websites, it has its drawbacks. For one thing, using this method means that the bookmarks are tied to the computer on which they were originally stored. Second, if you want to share a website with someone, you must copy the site's address and paste it into an email message, a blog posting, or a comment on the other person's social networking page.

Fortunately, there is a much simpler, more effective, and more advanced way to keep track of and share those fascinating websites we find. This is where the "social" half of social bookmarking comes in. Using a service that resides on the Internet, one can share any information that is on the Web. This means the information is not tied down to a single computer but is attached to a user's account on a given provider. It is the same principle that is behind email storage, a system that allows the user to log in anywhere in the world and retrieve his or her messages. We are no longer tied down as much by location as by imagination!

The various social bookmarking services each have unique features that attract a particular type of user. But for the most part they offer a few common features, including online storage of bookmarked sites, rating systems, social interaction through a list of friends or an open community, and the ability to tag key words on websites. These key words can help future readers find information faster when they search for specific terms. For example, a website that has lots of information on different pages can have different tags on specific pages to help people locate information. Like everything in the Web 2.0 movement, most social bookmarking services offer profile pages that can be customized and browser plug-ins or add-ons for seamless integration. These features are designed to create a unique and streamlined Web experience.

Let's take a look at three different social bookmarking options. Digg.com is a website that acts more like a news site. The top stories are dictated by the highest numbers of diggs. Huh? Stay with us here. As we mentioned, some services provide rating systems. Digg.com uses "diggs" as a measuring unit to keep track of how many users "digg" a certain news item or webpage. The site's users choose what news items are interesting, and in doing so become part of a community with similar interests. Being able to have this type of freedom to determine what information is relevant gives online users a new voice. How could this help in a classroom environment? Digg maintains a searchable database of articles that have been "dugg." A search for "Health Care Reform" returns with various news articles that have users' ratings attached to them. This type of research can help a student acknowledge the different points of view regarding any given matter.

While digg.com focuses more on news items and the accumulation of users' votes, delicious.com sticks to a truer bookmarking experience. It too offers its own type of rating system, which is based on the number of people who have bookmarked a specific page. Easing the switch from an old-school, if you will, style of storing bookmarks on a single computer, delicious.com offers the ability to import bookmarks to its site and tag them. This enables users to keep their beloved bookmarks, tag them accordingly for organization, and share them with the world. Delicious.com is a barebones-style website that focuses on the content rather than outside, irrelevant distractions. Using this service can be a great way for students to begin their research, collect information, collaborate by sharing with one another, and finally compile a presentation.

Our last and perhaps most interesting recommendation is StumbleUpon (of course, there will be more of these types of tools developed every year). This service offers users smart suggestions for websites it thinks they might find interesting, based on criteria that they have preselected. Once users create an account at www.stumbleupon.com, they are asked to go through a list of categories and subcategories to choose what their interests are. They then use a StumbleUpon bar in their browser to "stumble" through random sites that the service suggests. While it might look trivial on the surface, there are more specific options and practices that can make the use of StumbleUpon more productive. A user can like or dislike a certain page, and the service learns from the user's choices for future suggestions. The user can also discover new pages and add them to the service's database. A specific category can be chosen if the user only wants to "stumble" sites that fall under it. Sharing and collaborating is easy through a send function that allows the user to send a website to another StumbleUpon user or anyone in his or her email list. The functionality offered by StumbleUpon can help a group of students tag, organize, and share from any computer in or outside of school.

All of these tools offer us a new way to search for information. It's not important to get caught up in the fancy visuals or the obscure terms, but it is important to know how to use these tools and to pass these practices on to our students, so that they can take full advantage of them.

Teaching Information to Find Students

An overlooked phenomenon in education is the use of Web 2.0 features that cause information to find the student. In truth, our exclusion of these tools in our classrooms relegates students to understanding only half of the power of digital information sources. These Web feed tools (sometimes called news feeds) continually search the Web for new postings related to a person's interest. In effect, these tools pull information on behalf of the subscriber to keep him or her updated on events. Most of us use these in our adult lives, perhaps by having gadgets installed on our home page that keep us informed about news events or by subscribing to the feeds from particular blogs and wikis. For example, Nancy uses a Web feed that notifies her whenever a new posting appears on a response to intervention wiki sponsored by the International Reading Association, while Doug is notified of new videos and reports produced by Edutopia, a nonprofit educational organization.

The most common Web feed tool is RSS (Really Simple Syndication). Many websites and blogs feature an RSS icon that invites you to subscribe so that new posts come to you, rather than having to search them out individually. An RSS subscription needs to go somewhere, however, so you must first sign up for a reader (think of it as a virtual notepad) that collects those Web feeds and holds on to them for you. The generic term for a reader is a Web-based aggregator, and the most widely known is Google Reader. Other Web-based aggregators include Bloglines and blogs.com, and many email systems have the functionality to collect Web feeds as well.

While students find social bookmarking useful for storing, tagging, and sharing websites, the information tagged is valid only on a specific site, and a user must check the site regularly to see any changes that have been posted. Using a website's RSS feed enables students to be notified as soon as there is an update. With some initial effort in the research stage of an assignment, students can benefit from this technology as their newsreaders are actively updated. If the students use an online service, such as Google Reader, the information follows them anywhere. We've often noticed how adolescents are glued to their cell phones. Whether it's reading a text or checking their favorite social networking site, they are connected 24/7. We can use this to our advantage, as there are newsreaders for mobile devices, including cell phones. Seems to be a trend, doesn't it? You find something, you like it, it follows you. No more need to keep track of various websites, and this is key to helping students stay on top of things. These types of technology not only help educate the student on a given subject, but they also teach him or her how to stay organized.

Take Andrew, for example, a student at our school. Among his various interests at age seventeen, his top two are homeopathic medicine and heavy metal music. While he explores alternative options in medical treatment, he can be damaging his hearing. Such are the extremes of an adolescent's interests. We offered Andrew the chance for both topics to meet in a single place, Google Reader. At first, Andrew seemed puzzled as to what we were showing him, but he came prepared with an open mind. Once he created an account with Google, essentially a Gmail account, we introduced him to the Google Reader page. Soon after we pointed out the search feature on the page, he was on his way to Googling for RSS feeds. This product offers RSS feeds cataloged by Google. Other applications offer the ability to search bookmarked pages and add their feeds, eliminating the step of manually subscribing via a page's RSS or Atom (a different feed format) icon. After searching for both homeopathic and alternative medicine, Andrew narrowed his search and subscribed to Dr. Weil's website (www.drweil.com). This site offered information on various alternative medicine topics that Andrew could research. Along with Dr. Weil's RSS feed, Andrew subscribed to a feed from a website dedicated to publishing heavy metal and other music news, blabbermouth.net. Although these sites are dedicated to very different subjects, being able to access their information from a single interface, anywhere in the world, attracted Andrew. His world just became a whole lot more accessible.

Andrew's introduction to RSS feeds serves as a precursor to what could become a powerful research habit. As with many of the tools offered and spoken about in this book, the most important consideration is not what the technology can do but how it is used. Collecting data is one thing, but creating actual information that is valuable and relevant is the goal.

Chapter Tweets

While the need to search for information is not new, the tools have changed since we were in school.

Wikipedia can be a useful means for beginning a search because it provides a broad overview of a topic.

Boolean terms serve a useful purpose in limiting searches and are widely used on databases.

Advanced search operators can further refine Web searches.

Locating information is a first step, but students also need to be taught how to verify and evaluate information.

Remember that information goes two ways in literacy 2.0. Utilize Web feeds to cause information to come to students.

Chapter 3

Using Information: Making Responsible Choices

It has been said that "liberty is always unfinished business," and nowhere is this truer than on the Internet. On the one hand, the largest number of people in human history have ready access to information. People across the world can read the works of Plato, St. Augustine, Confucius, Marx, Dickinson, Angelou, Gandhi . . . the possibilities are dizzying. Whether you agree or disagree with the ideas themselves, there exists the possibility that people can make judgments for themselves, without the layers of interpreters who can change the message. On the other hand, the largest number of people in human history have ready access to an audience. Hate groups, fundamentalists who preach violence, extremists who advocate for the dismantling of all social orders . . . the possibilities are dizzying. Without the layers of interpreters who can balance the message and question invalid claims, people are vulnerable to dangerous misinformation that hurts other people.

Now throw an impressionable and impetuous adolescent into the mix. She may lack the background knowledge she needs to temper those invalid claims, as well as the healthy skepticism needed to recognize and question unsupported claims. Heap on the naïveté of young people (who are pretty sure they invented everything anyway), and you've got a potential victim in the making.

But this knife cuts both ways. This adolescent is also capable of putting a lot of junk out there. Let's face it, there's a reason that societies don't put fourteen-year-olds in charge. The kinds of things that in past generations had a limited audience are now out there for the world to consume. Gossip isn't just whispered in the school hallway—it's written on a MySpace page. A foolish choice doesn't fade with memory—it is sent to an entire address book on a cell phone. Half-baked ideas about the world don't fall on the ears of a few tolerant friends who gently ignore you—they are posted on a blog where billions (theoretically) can read them.

The social complexities of adolescence can certainly be exacerbated by the availability of technological tools that make it too easy to hit "send" before thinking through the consequences. Parents know that raising young people to make responsible and ethical decisions can be challenging. But let's take it a step further: what are schools doing to educate students to make responsible and ethical decisions?

Responsible and ethical decision making is influenced in equal parts by a worldview and by personal experiences. In other words, "think globally, act locally." Much has been made of issues such as Internet safety, cyberbullying, sexting (sending provocative photos via text messages), and the like. There is no question that these issues are important and that we should be paying attention to them. But we also have to ask whether our curriculum is sufficiently geared toward teaching decision making. If learning is defined by the ability to regurgitate information, we leave students vulnerable to a naïve acceptance of what is placed before them. And if teaching is measured as the ability to deliver information, we leave teachers vulnerable to becoming unthinking automatons. For us, these concerns lie at the nexus of literacy and citizenship. A literacy 2.0 curriculum teaches decision making by ensuring that students have lots of opportunities to think critically and then act upon their choices. And it allows teachers to use their wisdom to guide young people as they build their habits of mind.

Citizenship and Literacy 2.0

As we have noted in previous chapters, the net effect of the 'Net has been to shrink the distance we have between one another. While this development increases the possibility of a free exchange of ideas, it appears that there is less exchange than ever, at least when it comes to people with differing views. One need only turn on a television to find the talking heads of the like-minded reciting talking points that sound eerily similar. Rarely do these so-called discussions include people with other views, and when they do the discourse seems to devolve into a game of simply shouting one another down. Check out a blog or the comments left on a website, and you'll find the same phenomenon, just a different tool.

At the same time, teachers across the country are trying to foster a very different atmosphere in their classrooms. In doing so, they are taking an approach to citizenship education that extends beyond the conventional walls of civics education. Whether teaching English, or mathematics, or any other content, they want to impress upon their students that a rational exchange of ideas is essential. Democratic ideals are not the sole purview of the history department;

they should be taught every day, in every classroom. A democracy depends on it, pure and simple.

The Center for Information on Civic Learning and Engagement (CIRCLE), a nonpartisan research center located at Tufts University, studied how various themes emphasized in social studies, history, and civics courses affected young people ages fifteen to twenty-five. The researchers found that the 30 percent of their sample who had participated in courses in which the major theme was "great American heroes and virtues" were "more trusting," an arguably dangerous attitude in a complex world (Levine & Lopez, 2004). The 9 percent whose courses had emphasized a critical examination of social injustices, such as racism, were more likely to vote and to become involved in community-based problem solving. These findings suggest that a classroom that invites a critical analysis of a democratic system yields a more engaged citizenry. Importantly, the freedom offered by a democracy allows students to engage in this type of critical analysis and to freely exchange ideas, a point learners need to return to over and over again.

This exchange of ideas is also at the heart of literacy instruction. Rosenblatt (1938/1994) wrote of the transactions between reader and text as a "shaping process" that changes the reader through the act of experiencing it (p. 133). She went on to state that these transactions are particular to the individual and are influenced by a person's knowledge, experience, and purpose for reading. This is what makes book club discussions so interesting. If everyone held the exact same opinion about a book, it wouldn't be very interesting. Most of us who belong to a book club do so because we actively enjoy the transactional nature of reading and the differences it evokes among people.

In the first decade of the 21st century, researchers and educators in Australia and New Zealand led a shift in literacy instruction to an approach called *critical literacy*. The Tasmania (Australia) Department of Education (2007) explains that "critical literacy involves the analysis and critique of the relationships among texts, language, power, social groups and social practices. It shows us ways of looking at written, visual, spoken, multimedia and performance texts to question and challenge the attitudes, values and beliefs that lie beneath the surface." To help students in our classes develop critical literacy, we regularly remind them to:

1. Question the Commonplace in a Text

2. Consider the Role of the Author

3. Seek Alternative Perspectives

4. Read Critically (Frey, Fisher, & Berkin, 2008, p. 111)

Critical literacy demands that the reader deliberately assume a stance that takes other viewpoints into account. This is a central tenet of citizenship: the ability to advocate for an improved community, and not just for the part of the community that is exactly like you. Hess (2009) writes, "There is an intrinsic and crucial connection between the discussion of controversial political issues, especially among people with disparate views, and the health of a democracy. This is because participating in political discussion can have two powerful effects: it makes people more politically tolerant and it causes them to learn more about important issues" (p. 12).

A literacy 2.0 curriculum allows for the discussion of ideas in speech and in writing and uses critical literacy to promote citizenship. Through content and instruction, it teaches students to make responsible and ethical decisions. And it capitalizes on the breathtaking access to information that we enjoy today. Give students opportunities to study the decisions of others, because it helps them to learn how to make decisions for themselves.

Becoming a Citizen Through the Stories of Others

The experiences of those we meet in fiction and nonfiction can shed light on our own lives. As educators, we expose our students to the lives of others through biography and autobiography, poetry, realistic fiction, and fantasy. Not every genre appears in every discipline; however, schooling at its best is an act of introducing the sweep of intellectual thought throughout human history. Indeed, a duty of every generation is to carry forward the experiences of its elders. In societies with an oral tradition, this is done through story and song. In print-based societies, this is done through written texts.

In our own practice, we ask our students two questions that serve as an informal means of examining the experiences of others in the books they read. The first question we ask students to consider is: *How do multiple perspectives enhance and inhibit the practice of freedom?* This is a direct extension of a critical literacy stance that is vital for 21st century citizenship because it reminds students that understanding the viewpoints of others is a necessary component of responsible and ethical decision making. The second question is intended to move the students to action: *What is our responsibility as citizens to preserve the freedoms of others?* While these questions are not easily answered (a characteristic of an essential question), we find that adolescents are eager to explore topics that defy a simple explanation. Fortunately, the world is filled with texts that invite introspection and discussion.

Texts That Examine Personal Freedom

The topic of personal freedom is an important one, particularly for middle school students, who are facing newfound personal freedoms of their own that sometimes challenge their ability to make responsible choices. We also think it's helpful for students to face difficult choices through the characters they meet in books before they have to do so in their own lives, so that they can draw on these vicarious experiences if needed in the future.

One of our current favorites is *The Absolutely True Diary of a Part-Time Indian*, by Sherman Alexie (2007), a fictional memoir based on the author's experiences as a Native American living on a reservation in Washington. When the protagonist, Arnold "Junior" Spirit, is offered a chance to attend Reardon High School in town, he takes it. However, the duality of his identities—too "white" for the rez, too Indian for Reardon—leaves him feeling as though he has a foot in two worlds without fully belonging to either. Junior must cope with death in the family, the anger of a former best friend, and a romance with a Caucasian girl at his school. Although Junior tries to compartmentalize his life, these conflicts collide in a basketball game near the end of the story. Junior's struggle to find his identify morphs into a new and more complex definition of self as he learns to negotiate multiple identities.

Although the book is contemporary, the issues it raises are timeless. In the chapter "Valentine Heart," Junior makes a connection to a quotation by Euripides: "What greater grief than the loss of one's native land?" (Alexie, 2007, p. 173). After posing the question "Who the heck was Euripides?" we invite students to learn about the ancient Greek playwright by conducting a Web search. After they learn about the playwright, we ask them to consider why this quote has such meaning to Junior.

Middle school students sometimes dream of a world in which all the seemingly restrictive rules that impinge on their fun vanish. As adults, we like to remind them that the rules are there for a reason, but this is not always deeply appreciated by the young. Many of us remember reading *Lord of the Flies* (Golding, 1959) when we were in school and being introduced to the perils of a society wiped clean of rules. However, the violence and cruelty of that story can be difficult for some readers, who may not yet be able to understand the allegorical nature of the tale. We've since added another novel to our collection—*How I Live Now*, by Meg Rosoff (2004). This title is a bit more accessible for middle school readers. It chronicles the experiences of a fifteen-year-old girl named Daisy who lives in the near future. While she is visiting relatives in England during her summer vacation, the nation is invaded, and Daisy finds herself stranded in a farmhouse with no adults. She and her cousins initially create their own world, which is soon interrupted by soldiers who send them off to a work camp. The first-person narration feels intimate as Daisy struggles to find out who she is, now that she has been changed by these events. "Every war has turning points, and every person, too," Daisy foretells (p. 68). We ask students to track the changes in the character from before the war, especially the irony of having an eating disorder that foreshadows the threat she will later face of starvation through deprivation. One former student of ours, who also struggled with an eating disorder, told the class about the need for feeling in control of something when everything else seems chaotic. Her insights about Daisy's internal and external battles for personal freedom cast a new light on the motivations of the main character.

Texts That Examine Social Injustice

To understand how injustice can occur in other places across the world, one must first understand how it can occur within our midst. The enslavement of African Americans is a prime example for study. This subject is well covered in young adult literature, and one excellent source that has endured is *To Be a Slave*, by Julius Lester (2000). The text is based on slave narratives that were collected between 1936 and 1938 as part of the Federal Writers' Project, which was operated by the Works Progress Administration during the Depression era. Writers, many by that time elderly themselves, crisscrossed the country to record the memories of formerly enslaved people. Students explore the online collection of the Library of Congress (http://memory.loc.gov/ammem/snhtml), which includes 2,300 slave narratives and 500 photographs. Not only do we want our students to learn how primary source documents are accessed and interpreted, but we also want them to understand how this project represented an attempt to right the wrongs of previous generations by capturing these stories so that such grievous errors would not be repeated.

The issue of blame is a complicated one, as is the need for groups to assign blame to others. Responsible and ethical decision making requires that assigning well-deserved blame does not lapse into scapegoating. We ask high school students to examine the psychology of scapegoating in order to understand how this phenomenon can factor into historical and contemporary events. Students begin by reading and discussing the short story "The Lottery," by Shirley Jackson (1948/2005), a chilling account of a small town's annual ritual of stoning one of its own citizens to death. We invite the students to examine why the author spends time describing the black box that contains the names of all the residents. They discuss the sentence that comes near the end, just before townspeople stone Tessie Hutchinson: "Although the villagers had forgotten the ritual and lost the original black box, they still remembered to use stones." Our discussion usually focuses on the excuse heard so often in other circumstances: "That's the way we've always done it." One of the intended outcomes of this unit is to encourage students to evaluate the role of traditions in perpetuating injustices.

Students extend their understanding of the role of blame by reading *The Devil on Trial* (Margulies & Rosaler, 2008). The book examines five trials: the Salem witch trials of 1692–93, the Haymarket bomb trial of 1886, the Scopes trial of 1926, the Alger Hiss trials of 1949–50, and the Zacarias Moussaoui trial after the September 11 attacks. The complexities of these five trials don't allow students to distance themselves from the decisions. While the witch trials were clearly an injustice, other trials were the result of real crimes. The most provocative is the Zacarias Moussaoui trial, which resulted in a life sentence in the Supermax prison facility in Colorado. These terrible events happened within the students' memory, and all have strong feelings about them. The Moussaoui trial serves as a foil to the others as the students come to understand the need at times for assigning blame. The intended outcome of this unit is to understand the role of blame—sometimes misplaced, sometimes justified—and the need to proceed cautiously when making such decisions.

Texts That Examine Controversial Topics

Adolescents have a well-deserved reputation for their willingness to debate nearly anything, and asking them to examine controversial topics capitalizes on this developmental need. In our efforts to teach students argumentation (not arguing), we deliberately place topics in front of them that don't have pat answers. Fortunately and unfortunately, our world is filled with many such topics. The intent of this approach is to foster a healthy skepticism balanced by deep knowledge and a desire to always ask, "What if?" For us, the ability to ask such questions, seek out answers, and form judgments lies at the heart of literacy 2.0.

Because our high school has a health sciences focus, we introduce students to controversial topics through a ninth-grade course on legal and ethical issues in health care. The course culminates with an assignment to write an analytic research paper. Students are given a variety of topics to choose from, including euthanasia, stem cell research, abortion, cloning, and assisted suicide. Throughout the semester they have been learning about how laws, ethics, and morals influence the health profession. They have also learned about credible sources, citing the works of others, and the structure of an analytic research paper (see fig. 3.1, page 56, for a sample assignment). After they choose a topic, we meet with them to discuss print and online resources. For example, students might read *The Ethics of Human Cloning* (Kass & Wilson, 1998), watch an online video on research and animal rights from the University of San Diego, or listen to a podcast from Stanford on the ethics of stem cell research. The biggest challenge for most students is that they want to discuss only one position (theirs) and would rather not acknowledge the criticisms of detractors. Therefore, we require that they explore and use credible sources both for and against their chosen health issue. Students do not report their opinion in this analytic research paper; instead, the purpose of this assignment is to examine both sides of an issue they are likely to feel strongly about.

What Is an "Analytic Research Paper"?

An analytic research paper highlights a particular issue or problem. The paper focuses on analysis of the issue and its solutions. The posture of the writer is that of a neutral observer more than an advocate for a particular position. The success of the paper is based on how completely and clearly the writer has identified the key aspects of the issue and the significance to the field to which they relate.

Your analytic paper is about a controversial issue in the health care field, and you will choose the topic you would like to research. We encourage you to talk with your family about what you are learning, and to find out what they think about the topic. This will help you to understand the complexities of the moral arguments for and against the issue you have selected. Suggested topics include:

- Stem cell research
- Assisted suicide
- Euthanasia
- Choosing your baby's gender and/or other traits ("designer babies")
- Genetic engineering
- Gene therapy
- Cloning
- Abortion
- Assisted fertilization
- Gender reassignment surgery
- Adoption by gay couples
- Reporting genetic health risks to employers and insurance companies
- Others?

Here are the quick facts about your analytic research paper:

1. The paper includes complete and factual information about each of these three elements: Legal Aspects, Professional Ethics, and Moral Arguments For and Against.

2. Each of these elements is supported by at least two credible sources of information (book, encyclopedia, website).

Figure 3.1: Assignment sheet for analytic research paper.

3. A Works Cited page contains each of these sources, using MLA style.

4. The paper is typed, double-spaced, in Times or Times New Roman font (12 pt.); it is 2–4 pages in length, not counting the Works Cited page.

5. The paper contains title, author's name (yours), and headings to organize it.

6. The work is original, and your own.

Texts That Examine a Call to Action

In addition to exposing students to the experiences of others, we want to move them to take action of their own. Although otherwise confident, many adolescents find it difficult to figure out how they can effect positive change. One of the best role models for middle school readers is Hunter Scott, whose story is told in *Left for Dead: A Young Man's Search for Justice for the USS Indianapolis* (Nelson, 2002). Eleven-year-old Hunter chose the *USS Indianapolis* disaster of World War II for his sixth-grade social studies fair project. Hunter first learned about the sinking of this ship while watching the movie *Jaws*. The tragedy is well known because after the ship was attacked by a torpedo, 880 sailors spent four days in the waters off Palau, where many of them died from exposure and shark attacks. The ship's sinking was not known about for days, both because of gross mismanagement of the distress signals that were sent and because the ship was on a secret mission to deliver parts to be used in the atomic bombing of Nagasaki a few weeks later. The captain, Charles McVay, was court-martialed and convicted, even though many survivors did not agree with the findings. He committed suicide in 1968.

Hunter interviewed survivors and learned of their belief that the captain had been wrongly court-martialed. The middle school student began a personal campaign to have the case reopened and contacted Navy officials and politicians. The media learned about his efforts, and eventually Hunter testified before the Senate Armed Services Committee. Congress finally exonerated the captain in 2000.

Stories like Hunter Scott's are rare, and we want to make sure that our students know that taking action starts with the choices they make in their own lives. *The Pact: Three Young Men Make a Promise and Fulfill a Dream* (Davis, Jenkins, & Hunt, 2002) is an example of the outcomes of positive choices. The authors made a pact just before entering high school that they would help one another become doctors. The story is all the more remarkable because the young men's economic and educational circumstances were not in their favor. However, the three teens from Newark, New Jersey, made it through high school and college together, and today two are medical doctors, while the third is a dentist. They have established the Three Doctors Foundation (www .threedoctorsfoundation.org) to mentor other young people. After reading the book, students learn about this outreach project and set up their own online accounts with the University of California and California State University systems. In addition, they write and upload résumés to a scholarship search service our school uses to support their postsecondary goals. They learn about the Common Application, a membership organization of nearly 400 colleges and universities that streamlines the application process through its website, https://www.commonapp.org. Much like the authors of *The Pact,* these students learn that setting goals is an important, but not the only, step in achieving success. They must take concrete actions that move them closer to realizing their goals.

Helpful Resources

Locating thought-provoking texts can be a time-consuming project, especially when trying to find newer titles. There are several resources we use regularly to keep up on what's available. The Read Write Think website, a collaborative project of the International Reading Association and the National Council of Teachers of English, features a series of podcasts on compelling young adult literature. The series, titled Text Messages, features discussions about books that our students find interesting. You can listen to the podcasts online at www.readwritethink.org (visit go.solution-tree.com/literacy for the complete URL for the podcasts). In addition, you can subscribe for free to the Text Messages series through iTunes. We have our students listen to short podcasts like these in order to gain a sense of how discussions about books sound.

The awards section of the American Library Association is a helpful website for locating notable books for young adults (www.ala.org/ala/awardsgrants/ index.cfm). Awards of special interest include the Sibert Medal for best informational books, the Printz Award for excellence in young adult literature, and the Young Adult Library Services Association awards for audiobooks.

Reading about and discussing how fictional characters and real people make ethical and responsible decisions is an important part of becoming a citizen of the 21st century. But we know that we must move students to apply these principles in their own lives. As teachers, we can have the most influence over students' decision making in their academic lives. Technological advances complicate decisions in that realm, particularly when it comes to issues of plagiarism. Figuring out what plagiarism means in a digital age is another element of a literacy 2.0 curriculum.

Making Responsible and Ethical Decisions in Writing: Plagiarism

It seems that with every technological advancement, there is a new crime waiting to happen. And so it is with plagiarism in the 21st century. The rise of digital resources has made plagiarism easier than ever, in large part because long passages can be copied and pasted into documents. For the more unscrupulous, hundreds of websites selling papers have sprouted up like mushrooms. With increased technological availability have come all those dire reports about the plagiarism rampant in education and the futile efforts of teachers and administrators to stop it. The plagiarism detection industry is growing exponentially, with TurnItIn (http://turnitin.com) boasting 500,000 users. The voices that call for better teaching as the solution are drowned out by talk of honor codes and threats of expulsion for academic dishonesty.

While we recognize that there are cases that need to be dealt with through sanctions, our experience is that the vast majority of students who plagiarize do so because they lack the sophistication to do otherwise. At our school, students suspected of plagiarizing meet with Nancy to discuss what happened. In nearly every case, they fall into one or more of the following categories:

1. Those who don't know how to properly cite

2. Those who don't know when to properly cite

3. Those who don't know enough about the topic

4. Those who waited too long to get started on an assignment and panicked

Let that list sink in for a moment. Consider the times when you have confronted a student who was suspected of plagiarizing—would any of these descriptions fit? Certainly the first three issues should be addressed through academics. (We would argue that the fourth is at least related to academics.) And yet in most schools, the official plagiarism policy begins and ends with a catalog of consequences. We'll pose the same question we asked earlier in this chapter: what are we as educators doing to teach our students how to make responsible and ethical decisions? Michele Eodice, director of the University of Oklahoma Writing Center, wonders "why we would choose punishment over pedagogy" when our job is to teach (2008, p. 17). Gilmore (2008) goes even further: "Once a teacher is reduced to the role of source detective, he has already lost the educational battle" (p. 5).

As a school we have struggled with how best to respond to plagiarism cases, and we suspect we are not the only ones who find ourselves in the weeds on this matter. It is also fair to say that dealing with plagiarism has detracted from our central mission to educate students, and we have had to spend time repairing the damaged relationships between students, teachers, and families. Teachers feel duped, students feel cornered, and parents feel shame when the act occurs. Our response has been to develop and teach a department-wide unit on plagiarism in every English class, every year. Teachers in the other content areas have access to the unit as well (via Google Docs) and reinforce principles from it in their classes. We have posted a style guide on the e-platform for every student in the school so that the correct forms for citation and referencing are available at any time of the day or night. And most importantly, we teachers demonstrate accepted academic practices in our own work. Our instructional materials need to be properly attributed so that students are continually exposed to the correct forms. To make our practices transparent, we discuss these references with our classes. Many teachers use a think-aloud process to model how they make decisions about citing these materials. Simply stated, we can't teach proper attribution just as part of the research paper assignment and then forget about it for the rest of the term.

Inspired by the work of Vosen (2008) and the plagiarism unit she uses with her university students, we set out to design a similar approach for ensuring that all the students at our school learn about plagiarism in their English classes during the first weeks of school. We use the gradual release of responsibility model of instruction discussed in chapter 1 (Fisher & Frey, 2008a) to organize learning in these classes.

Lesson 1: What Is Plagiarism? Why Is It a Problem?

We begin by activating and building the students' background knowledge through the introduction of targeted vocabulary. We explain that *plagiarism* comes from the Greek word *plaga*, meaning to capture or trap, and remind the students of related terms such as *plague* (a fast-spreading and deadly disease) and *Las Plagas* (fictional parasitic species in the *Resident Evil 4* video game). Many students speak Spanish as a first or second language, so we also use the cognate *plagio*. Our final term for this lesson is *unauthorized,* which contains the affixes *un-* (not) and *-ize* (to become, which turns a noun into a verb). We point out that *authority* is the root word.

After introducing the day's vocabulary, we open up a discussion about unauthorized uses of ideas. These include:

- Sampling in music—Vanilla Ice samples the David Bowie/Queen song "Under Pressure" in his song "Ice, Ice, Baby." We play a portion of both of these songs so the students can hear the similarities.

- Knock-offs in fashion—We show the class photographs of real and knock-off versions of Louis Vuitton bags.

⬛ Overseas counterfeit prescription drugs—The Food and Drug Administration estimates that in some countries, up to 30 percent of prescription drugs sold are unauthorized copies. In the U.S., it is estimated to be 1 percent.

In each of these examples, there is someone who is harmed. Students are encouraged to discuss several questions, including identifying the victim in each case, the ways that person or organization is harmed, and the consequences for the person or organization that has committed fraud.

After this opening activity, we develop a K-W-L chart with students to find out what they already know about plagiarism. Possible responses might include knowing that there is a section in the student handbook on plagiarism, having been taught about paraphrasing in previous English classes, or knowing that plagiarism can result in a failing grade for an assignment.

Next, we show students the definition of plagiarism on Wikipedia and conduct a shared reading of the first paragraph of the complete entry. Using a think-aloud to model during the reading, we demonstrate how we understand the compare/contrast text structure, which includes a discussion of plagiarism in academic and journalistic circles, as well as new kinds of plagiarism that have arisen with digital sources. The Wikipedia entry begins as follows:

> Plagiarism, as defined in the 1995 *Random House Compact Unabridged Dictionary*, is the "use or close imitation of the language and thoughts of another author and the representation of them as one's own original work." Within academia, plagiarism by students, professors, or researchers is considered academic dishonesty or academic fraud and offenders are subject to academic censure. In journalism, plagiarism is considered a breach of journalistic ethics, and reporters caught plagiarizing typically face disciplinary measures ranging from suspension to termination. Some individuals caught plagiarizing in academic or journalistic contexts claim that they plagiarized unintentionally, by failing to include quotations or give the appropriate citation. While plagiarism in scholarship and journalism has a centuries-old history, the development of the Internet, where articles appear as electronic text, has made the physical act of copying the work of others much easier. (Plagiarism, 2010)

We now read aloud the following plagiarized version of the plagiarism entry, which we tell students we wrote ourselves:

> Plagiarism is the close imitation of another person's ideas, words, language, and thoughts. A person who plagiarizes is representing them as their own original work. This is considered academic dishonesty or academic fraud and anyone who does it can be punished. Sometimes people claim that they plagiarized unintentionally, either by failing to use quotes or citations. The development of the Internet, where there are articles in electronic text, has made copying the text of others much easier.

We ask the students for comments on this passage, expecting that they will tell us that it is plagiarized. When they do, we probe for specific examples to support the accusation, such as extended phrases taken from the original. We then invite a student to type one of these phrases into the Google search engine, using quotation marks, and the Wikipedia entry should turn up near the top of the list. We were inspired by Vosen (2008) to show our students how easily we can find plagiarized work on the Internet.

Having made the point that a plagiarized work can be easily detected, we next model writing while thinking aloud again. We write a short passage about plagiarism in front of the students, thinking aloud as we go to show them how we make decisions about word choice and major concepts. We finish this with the correct MLA citation for the entry:

> "Plagiarism." *Wikipedia: The Free Encyclopedia.* 12 August 2008. <http://en.wikipedia.org/wiki/Plagiarism>

The final portion of this first lesson is devoted to collaborative reading. We divide the class into small groups of three to five students and ask them to read and discuss one of the selected readings about plagiarism. The readings are differentiated for a range of readers:

- Average difficulty—"Circleville Valedictorian Steps Down After Admitting He Plagiarized Commencement Speech" (Nowak, 2008)

- More difficult—"An Education in the Dangers of Online Research" (Kinzie, 2008)

- Less difficult—"Naperville H.S. Principal Fired for Plagiarism" (Puccinelli, 2008)

Each group will give a brief summary of its article to the whole class. To help the students create their summaries, we give them a note-taking guide (fig. 3.2), which also asks for bibliographical information about the articles. We collect the filled-in guides so that we can return them to the students for a later lesson on writing references and in-text citations. We then conclude the lesson with an exit slip or partner discussion, asking students to summarize the key points they learned about plagiarism in that day's class.

Lesson 2: How Does Plagiarism Apply to My Schoolwork?

We begin this lesson with a lighthearted YouTube video that serves as an anticipatory activity and gets students talking. The video, titled "Before He Cheats: A Teacher's Parody" (McKenzie, 2007), is a clever take on a popular song. After reviewing terms from the previous lesson, we conduct a shared reading using the school's Code of Academic Integrity from the student handbook. We then compare this to the Wikipedia entry used in the previous lesson,

Note-Taking Guide

Name: _____ **Date:** _____ **Period:** _____

Directions: Read and discuss the plagiarism article assigned to your group. Take notes on the information about the article. Summarize the article so that your group can report out to the class.

Author: _____

Title of Article: _____

Source: _____

Date of Publication: _____

Who was involved? _____

Position or Role: _____

What is he or she accused of doing? _____

_____

_____

What happened as a result? _____

_____

For a Future Lesson:

How would you write this for your Works Cited page?

How would you write this as an in-text citation?

Figure 3.2: Collaborative reading note-taking guide.

and students note the common elements in the descriptions of plagiarism, including the lack of full acknowledgment of the source. In addition, we point out the examples of plagiarism given in the handbook and discuss each one.

Next we use a collaborative learning activity inspired by the University of Leeds (n.d.) lesson called the Plagiarism Game. Students work in groups of four or five to consider various scenarios that may or may not constitute plagiarism. The scenarios are written out on notecards, and the students must discuss and come to consensus on each one. They record their decisions on a single worksheet with all of their names on it, explaining why each scenario is or is not an example of plagiarism (see fig. 3.3). We collect the groups' response sheets to make decisions about what needs to be taught in future lessons.

Is It Plagiarism?

Names of Group Members: _____

_____

Date: _____   Period: _____

Example	Yes or No?	Why?
1. Copying a paragraph from a book without acknowledging the author		
2. Taking a crib sheet into an exam		
3. Failing to put the word count on the front page of your essay		
4. Using exact text from another source for most of your essay, but including in-text citations and references		
5. Cutting and pasting a paragraph from an article with a few changes in word order, not putting the paragraph in quotation marks, but giving a reference both in text and in the bibliography.		
6. Making up quotations and references		
7. Working together with a friend to get ideas about the structure for an individual essay, then writing up the essays individually		
8. Taking short phrases from several sources and combining them with phrases of your own to compose a paragraph in your essay; including the references in the bibliography but not referencing them in the paragraph itself		

Figure 3.3: Plagiarism worksheet.

Example	Yes or No?	Why?
9. Copying another student's coursework with his or her knowledge		
10. Obtaining and using an essay from a previous year's student		
11. Stealing another student's essay and submitting it as your own		
12. Making up references to put in the bibliography		
13. Lending another student your work to look at		
14. Suggesting some useful references to a friend who is struggling with an essay		
15. Copying a few sentences from a textbook and putting them in your essay in quotation marks, referenced both in text and on the Works Cited page		

Source: Adapted from University of Leeds (n.d.). Used with permission.

Lesson 3: Mastering When and How to Cite

We begin by introducing new target vocabulary that will be used in this lesson. Because we want to both activate and build background knowledge about the terms, we discuss the following word origins, cognates, and structural elements:

- *Citation* comes from the Latin word *citare*, meaning to summon or move.

- *Citar* is the Spanish cognate for *citation*.

- *Paraphrase* can be structurally analyzed by breaking it down into *para-* (near or beside) and *phrase* (a group of words).

- *Para* is a false cognate in Spanish (means "stop" or "for").

We then introduce an activity called You Be the Judge. Students often have difficulty recognizing what needs to be cited and when. To help them learn to make the right decisions, we start by showing them the following passage from a website called Did You Know? (http://didyouknow.org):

> A diamond is the hardest natural substance on earth, but if it is placed in an oven and the temperature is raised to about 763 degrees Celsius (1405 degrees Fahrenheit), it will simply vanish, without even ash remaining. Only a little carbon dioxide will have been released.
>
> Diamonds are formed over a period of a billion or more years deep within earth's crust—about 150km (90 miles) deep—and [are] pushed to the surface by volcanoes. Most diamonds are found in volcanic rock, called Kimberlite, or in the sea after having been carried away by rivers when they were pushed to the surface.
>
> A diamond is 58 times harder than the next hardest mineral on earth, corundum, from which rubies and sapphires are formed. It was only during the 15th century that it was discovered that the only way to cut diamonds was with other diamonds. Yet, diamonds are brittle. If you hit one hard with a hammer, it will shatter. ("Diamond Facts," n.d.)

After the students read the passage, we give them the following series of statements and ask them to decide if they would have to give a citation if they used them in a paper:

- A diamond is the hardest substance in the world, and if you put it in an oven at 1405 degrees, it will disappear. [Answer: Yes]

- A diamond is 58 times harder than the next hardest mineral on earth, corundum, from which rubies and sapphires are formed. [Answer: Yes—needs quotation marks]

- A diamond is the hardest gem in the world. [Answer: No—common knowledge]

- A diamond is so brittle that if you hit it hard with a hammer, it will break into many small pieces. [Answer: Yes]

- Many people consider diamonds to be the most beautiful gem on Earth. [Answer: No—unrelated to this passage]

After finishing the guided instruction on whether a statement needs to be cited or not, we remind students of the tale of Hansel and Gretel and the breadcrumbs they left to mark a trail through the woods to find their way home. Students see the equivalent of this on their computers every day near the top of the screen. The navigation links that lead the students back to their original webpage are called a "breadcrumb trail." The in-text citations and the Works Cited section of a paper also work like a breadcrumb trail. The in-text citation leads the reader to the Works Cited page. Both items lead the reader to the original source.

We then return to the examples from the diamond entry used earlier in the lesson. Now that students have agreed on which statements need to be cited, we show them how to write a Works Cited reference for each, following MLA style. We point out that since the original source does not contain an author's name, we skip that element of the reference and begin with the title:

"Diamond Facts." *Did You Know?* 22 January 2010. <http://didyouknow. org/diamonds.htm>

Next we review the key points about the basics for in-text citations:

- Give only the information that is needed so that the reader can find the reference in your Works Cited section and can then find the original source.

- The in-text citation is inside parentheses and contains the author's name and the page number (print sources) or paragraph number (electronic source).

- If the Works Cited entry begins with the title (no author available), then use one or two key words from the title.

- Put the in-text citation as close to the information as possible (usually at the end of the sentence).

- Don't repeat information. If the author is mentioned in the sentence, then you only need the page number or paragraph number.

Now that students have agreed on which statements need to be cited, we show them how we write an MLA in-text citation for the examples used at the beginning of class:

- A diamond is the hardest substance in the world, and if you put it in an oven at 1405 degrees, it will disappear (Diamond, par. 1).

- "A diamond is 58 times harder than the next hardest mineral on earth, corundum, from which rubies and sapphires are formed" (Diamond, par. 2).

- A diamond is so brittle that if you hit it hard with a hammer, it will break into many small pieces (Diamond, par. 2).

We finish the lesson by distributing the note-taking guides that the students completed in the first lesson (fig. 3.2, page 63) and ask them to complete the Works Cited entry and in-text citation for the plagiarism article they read. We remind them to use the current day's date for the retrieval part of the record.

Lesson 4: Using Resources to Write Works Cited Entries

Memorizing the intricacies of MLA documentation requires regular exposure to correct examples, as well as frequent opportunities to write in-text citations and references in one's own work. We explain that most writers consult style sources to make sure they are composing these items correctly.

We begin by showing students two sources for use in this class. The first is a website a high school English teacher constructed for her own students (www.studyguide.org/MLAdocumentation.htm). We navigate the website and discuss how we locate information. We then explain that we have bookmarked this website on the classroom computers.

The second resource is the school's online style manual for students to consult when completing MLA documentation. We show students the table of contents and scroll through the handbook to locate information. We discourage students from printing this handbook (it is twenty-four pages long) and explain that we have loaded it onto the classroom computers and onto the e-platform for the class.

The remainder of the class is a partner activity that we call the MLA Scavenger Hunt, modeled on an activity designed by Vosen (2008). Using resources that can be found in the classroom, we ask students to work in pairs to locate the items listed on the worksheet and write a Works Cited entry for each one (see fig. 3.4).

MLA Scavenger Hunt

Names: _____ **Date:** _____ **Period:** _____

Directions: You must find a partner and cite works from the following categories. Remember, every period and comma counts! Even one character missing or misplaced denotes an incorrect answer. One pair will be crowned MLA Champions and will be awarded fantastic prizes. Good luck!

| 1. Book with one author |
| 2. Book with two or more authors |
| 3. An edition of a book |

Figure 3.4: MLA scavenger hunt.

4. An edited book
5. Work in an anthology
6. Encyclopedia entry
7. Newspaper article
8. Magazine article
9. Movie or TV program
10. CD
11. Interview
12. Website
13. Article on a website

Source: Adapted from Vosen (2008). Used with permission.

If the skills introduced in the plagiarism lessons were not revisited until the first research paper, due nine weeks later, it would be unlikely that much of the information that was taught would stick. The likelihood that students will integrate the ethical use of information into their own academic practices is dependent on whether their teachers continue to model how they locate and attribute sources. The bottom line is that learning how to make responsible and ethical decisions related to using information requires consistent exposure to people who do so themselves and who are willing to discuss their own decision-making processes. Students need lots of opportunities to pose questions about using information and then to act upon the answers they receive.

Chapter Tweets

Unprecedented access to information and an audience make digital advances both breathtaking and intimidating.

The interface between critical literacy and citizenship is an important element of literacy 2.0.

Rosenblatt's work on the transactions that occur between the reader and the text inform our understanding of literacy 2.0.

Students become 21st century citizens through the stories of others.

Look for texts that examine personal freedom, social injustices, and controversial topics and inspire a call to action.

Punishing plagiarism without investing in teaching is a lost cause. Instead, teach explicitly in order to prevent it from occurring.

Give students opportunities to make decisions in their own academic lives.

Chapter 4

Creating Information: Production in Literacy 2.0

"What's 'New Literacies'? What was wrong with the old ones?" We overheard this comment at a reading conference not too long ago and couldn't help but smile at the automatic assumption that new things always replace old things. While that may be true with some tools (after all, no one longs for an eight-track tape player), it is not true with functions. As we discussed in the introduction, the tools are going to continue to change with breathtaking speed. Even as we write this, we are fretting about our ability to keep current with technological developments. But we breathe a sigh of relief when we remind ourselves that the functions are timeless. The need to acquire, produce, and share information transcends the latest gadget or software.

New Literacies

Donald Leu and his colleagues acknowledge that new literacies (lowercase) can embrace a number of different areas, including informational literacy, discourse, reading comprehension, and learning strategies (Leu, O'Byrne, Zawilinski, McVerry, & Everett-Cacopardo, 2009). As they note, each of these new literacies (lowercase) draws from a variety of funds of knowledge that are informing our understanding as educators who are preparing learners in the 21st century. They offer four dimensions that collectively provide a working definition of New Literacies (uppercase):

1. New Literacies include the new skills, strategies, dispositions, and social practices that are required by new technologies for information and communication;

2. New Literacies are central to full participation in a global community;

3. New Literacies regularly change as their defining technologies change; and

4. New Literacies are multifaceted, and our understanding of them ben-
    efits from multiple points of view. (Leu et al., 2009, p. 266)

We see two common threads that weave through these elements, and both
have direct implications for the classroom. The first is that while technological tools present new opportunities for learners to engage with one another,
they should not be the tail that wags the dog but instead need to be continually
considered against the backdrop of "old" literacies: reading, writing, speaking, and listening. Second, the ready availability of technological tools makes it
imperative that we as educators abandon once and for all an outdated notion
of learners solely as receptacles of existing knowledge. In literacy 2.0, we need
to equip students with the cognitive tools that allow them to *produce and share*
knowledge—using sounds, images, and texts—and the technological tools that
provide them the means to do so. Students will still use their literacy 1.0 operating systems but will do so in new ways.

Podcasting: Creating With Voice and Video

Lexie sits in the corner of the room with her hood up and earbuds in her
ears while eight of her classmates are working on computers, a small group of
students are meeting with the teacher, five students are talking at a table about
their PowerPoint presentation, several students are reading in a classroom
library area, and several others seem to be working independently. The class is
abuzz with activity, some independent, some collaborative, and some guided by
the teacher. A visitor walking around the room and checking in with the students discovers that they are all working on history—the Industrial Revolution
and child labor laws, to be exact.

It is clear to the visitor that students in this classroom are engaged in a
range of experiences designed to deepen their understanding and that the
teacher doesn't feel the need to talk at students for hours on end. In asking the
teacher about the students' experiences, the visitor learns that this class period
started with the teacher showing a video called "Children in the Industrial
Revolution," which she found on TeacherTube (www.teachertube.com). This
video was just a few minutes long and was paired with an interesting song.
Following the video, the teacher modeled her thinking about the role of children and the jobs they were expected to do as well as why the creator of the
video would have selected the specific song. At the completion of her focus
lesson (see chapter 1), she reminded her students that their projects needed to
be uploaded on the course website during the week so that they could "go live"
for the whole school to see.

As you can imagine, the visitor was impressed with the overall operation
of the classroom and both *what* and *how* the students were learning. But the

visitor expressed concern about Lexie and her behavior, sitting in the corner listening to her MP3 player. She didn't seem to be "working," and the visitor questioned what she was getting out of the class.

Walking over to Lexie and asking her to pause her device and talk with him, the visitor learned that she was listening to a draft podcast that her group had made regarding child labor laws and the changes in the laws over the years. As Lexie said, "We've gotta get it edited so we sound professional and have the right info. Lots of people will hear this, and we want them to have accurate information." Yes, our assumptions about learning are challenged in classrooms that operate with a deep understanding of literacy 2.0.

So what is podcasting? Wikipedia describes a podcast as "a series of digital media files (either audio or video) that are released episodically and downloaded through web syndication" (Podcast, 2010). In other words, podcasts are sound or video files that can be shared with others. Most people have some experience with podcasts because iTunes provides a free service through which people can upload and share podcasts on a wide range of topics. The system operates via a subscription. When a user finds a podcast he or she likes, it's as simple as a click to subscribe, and then each time new content is added, the system grabs it and transfers it to the user's mobile device (MP3 player, iPod) when it is next connected. For example, National Public Radio often has the top podcast each week, and millions of people subscribe to this free service.

We ask our students to subscribe to the Classic Tales podcast. Each week, B. J. Harrison records a classic piece of literature and provides it free to all subscribers (for more information, see www.theclassictales.com). As we write this book, the current classic tales podcast is *Frankenstein*, which is spread over several weeks. Our colleagues have had students subscribe to podcasts from the History Channel, National Geographic, Science Daily, and various current events sites (such as ABC News, NBC News, and CNN).

Receiving information in this way builds students' background knowledge and provides an opportunity for the teacher to scaffold student learning. For example, Pak (2009) used podcasts with her students to develop their sophistication in writing. McDonald (2008) podcasts his physics lectures for students to access again and again, which allows them to develop deeper conceptual understandings.

There are many examples of using podcasts to convey content to students. But this chapter is about students producing information. And podcasts provide students with one way to share their thinking with a wide audience. That's just what the students in Lexie's group were doing. They created a podcast using the Audacity software program (http://audacitysourceforge.net). Audacity is free, open-source software for recording and editing sounds. It is available for Mac OS X, Microsoft Windows, GNU/Linux, and other operating systems. Using Audacity, students can:

- Record live audio
- Cut, copy, splice, or mix sounds together
- Change the speed or pitch of a recording
- Dub over existing tracks to create multitrack recordings
- Remove static, hiss, hum, or other constant background noises
- Import and export files

The great thing about Audacity is that, in addition to being free, it's very intuitive and students can use it immediately, with very little training required. In fact, most of our students already know how to edit because of iMovie or GarageBand and easily transition to editing using Audacity.

As part of their podcast, the students provided listeners with information about child labor laws in effect today. For example, Brian, one of the students in the group, explained,

> Minors, people under eighteen years of age, cannot do any work that the U.S. Department of Labor says is hazardous. These hazardous jobs usually involve excavation, mining, manufacturing explosives, and operating several types of power-driven equipment. Of course, some minors do these things at home with their family. Like, I've used a chain saw to cut trees, but my dad was there. The child labor laws say that I can't do this as a paid job.

When asked about their podcast, the members of Lexie's group indicated that they obtained information from a number of sources, including their textbook, the Internet (and specifically Wikipedia, the U.S. Department of Labor website, and www.stopchildlabor.org), and primary source documents such as contemporary political cartoons, editorials, newspaper articles, and interviews. Their podcast demonstrates their understanding of the content and their ability to use components of literacy 1.0 to create information that is consistent with literacy 2.0.

Of course, podcasts aren't limited to audio files. There are video podcasts (also called vodcasts or vidcasts), in which images are used in conjunction with spoken words. Video podcasts range from recorded PowerPoint presentations to full productions with video cameras and Photoshop editing. We recently had a student create a video podcast as part of her response to the essential question "Does age matter?" (A later section of this chapter will discuss essential questions in more detail.) In her video, Lapresha interviewed teenagers and adults about this question and compared and contrasted their responses. At the end of her video podcast, Lapresha offered her perspective on the question and concluded that age doesn't matter but maturity and responsibility do. Like Lexie and her group, Lapresha had to use a number of literacy 1.0 skills as well as literacy 2.0 skills to make her case. As is consistent with the concept of 2.0 applications, Lapresha's product was different from the product of any other student. It was hers and, as such, represented her thinking, her skills, and her understanding. As Knobel and Wilber (2009, p. 24) point out, "Literacy 2.0 means students take the reins," which is really the case when they create their own products and information.

Talking Pictures: Creating with Images

As we just noted, students often create with images. Images are powerful tools that communicate at both the conscious and subconscious levels. Just think about the use of images in commercials, political ads, and billboards. Marketing experts have long recognized the power of the image to communicate and persuade. Children also communicate through images and do so from the time they are very young. All parents of young children have a few of these images on their refrigerators and display them proudly as they recognize the cognitive processes required to create them.

Today, students can create images with more than crayons and paint. There are a host of tools available for creating and manipulating images. Some of these tools are quite expensive, and others are not. Sometimes they involve movie making, and other times they don't.

We'll start our foray into the use of images with a website that William Zimmerman developed to help students communicate through comics (www .makebeliefscomix.com). Students can use this site to create electronic comics that they can then save, print, or email to others. The site allows users to select from a number of characters, change the emotion of the character (which is a great teaching point in and of itself), add dialogue, and create a storyboard. One of Zimmerman's recommendations, which we have used, is to ask students to create an autobiographical comic strip about themselves and their families at the start of the year. While some students work on their introductory comics, others complete pre-assessment tasks, and others meet with the teacher to set goals for the year. We have found this activity to be a great way to start the year, as well as a way to communicate that we use technology tools in school as part of our learning. An example of a student's autobiographical comic appears in figure 4.1 (page 76, used with permission). Of course, Zimmerman's website can be used for more than student introductions. We've had students create comic strips about the books they've read, a colleague in math had students create comics demonstrating how to solve a specific problem, and a colleague in biology had students create comic strips about endangered species.

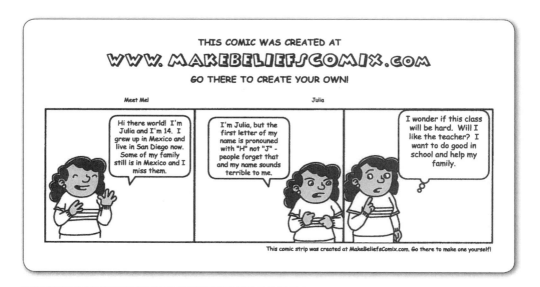

Figure 4.1: Julia's comic.

For a small fee, students can purchase a software program called ComicLife (available at http://plasq.com/comiclife) to create electronic comics. This program allows users to import photos and drawings as well as to create larger panels and pages. But the idea is still the same: students creating information with visuals (and words) that convey their understanding of the content. Our students also use GIMP (www.gimp.org), which is free, open-source software for image manipulation, photo retouching, and image authoring. They have become very skilled at image manipulation and now regularly question the images in textbooks.

Let's not forget that most mobile phones take reasonably good pictures, and many students own digital cameras. In other words, students can document their experiences with digital images and produce content with those images. The students in the earth science class are frequently outside, collecting samples and observing nature. They see tide pools, erosion, geologic records, mountains, and tons of other things all for free within a short ride of the school. Of course, their teacher also teaches them about the things they're seeing, and they do labs and other projects in class, including Internet research, but when they are in the field, they are required to document their findings visually. Students who do not have their own cameras share the school cameras. On a recent trip to the tide pools, the students documented the types of creatures that lived there, the times and tide levels, and the phase of the moon. They were all given information to look for but were encouraged to present it in a way that made sense to them.

Karen printed her photos on plain copy paper and created a photojournal of the experience. Brittney created a collage of her pictures using Photoshop and incorporated images from the Internet to add details. Javier developed a visual time line that documented the day and provided readers with details about the experience. Felicia posted her photos on Facebook and included commentary on each of them. Interestingly, other students from the class commented on Felicia's pictures, adding information and asking questions. Robert geotagged his photos, linked them with Google Earth, and wrote descriptors for each. Kim imported hers into PowerPoint, animated them, added background music, made audio recordings of information for each, and timed the transitions so that each photo would be seen while the information was relayed. Justin added his photos to his personal blog and wrote details about each picture. Again, these students used a number of literacy 1.0 processes and procedures to create usable information for both themselves and others. In doing so, they validated and extended their understanding of literacy 2.0 experiences.

Of course, students also have access to video recorders and really do love to record their world. Today, anyone with a few hundred dollars can make a movie. Just think about the explosion of content, much of it not very good, on YouTube. Really, how many times can you watch amateur skateboarders, dance recitals, and pranks? But there is something to be said for making movies. When we give students an opportunity to create with talking pictures, their imagination often soars, and they astound us with their creations.

In terms of tools for creating movies, we are most familiar with iMovie, as it is a fairly inexpensive and easy-to-use system for video editing (and comes free on new Apple computers). For PC users, Microsoft Movie Maker comes free on newer computers. Of course, there are much more professional systems available, such as Sony Vegas, Final Cut Pro, CyberLink PowerDirector, Corel VideoStudio, and Adobe Premiere.

As an example of making a movie as a classroom assignment, students in a biology class created video shorts about endangered species. They could collect stock footage or images or film the animals themselves (if they had access to their assigned animal). Their videos needed to include, at minimum, information about the animal, its habitat, why it was endangered, and what efforts were under way to prevent the animal from extinction. Students worked in groups of three to produce their videos. Mario, Brianna, and Omar focused their efforts on frogs. As they worked on their video, they learned that there are over one hundred types of frogs on the endangered species list and that Wikispecies has a complete taxonomy and searchable database. Their video introduces the topic, focuses on why frogs are endangered and threatened in different places in the world, and then profiles a few examples. As one of their examples, they showed a California red-legged frog (*Rana aurora draytonii*) and discussed an interview they did about the frog with a representative of the U.S. Fish and Wildlife Service. They noted that this frog was being protected in their hometown at the San Diego National Wildlife Refuge. Omar appears in the video, explaining the current recovery plans and petitions that have been filed to protect this particular frog.

This is just one example. There are hundreds of examples of students producing talking pictures as part of their efforts to create and understand content. The point is that students engage in content in different ways in classrooms that facilitate literacy 2.0. They're still learning the content and language but doing so in ways that are personally relevant and that give them opportunities to interact with ideas and others.

Access to an unprecedented amount of audio, visual, and textual information challenges us as educators to keep informed about the laws and guidelines governing classroom use of these materials. In particular, the legal definition of fair use in copyright law continues to evolve as technologies and literacies collide.

Fair Use

In the previous chapter, we discussed the importance of teaching students about plagiarism and its avoidance, focusing on how they can properly attribute the works and ideas of others. Unfortunately, experience has taught us that teaching about plagiarism can lead to overcompensation and breed fear among students and educators. In particular, the plagiarism unit usually triggers more questions about copyright law. First are the urban legend–style stories ("I heard about a teacher from Pennsylvania who was sent to prison for two years because she painted Disney characters on her classroom wall"). Next is the "err on the side of caution" mindset ("I'm not going to use anything in my classroom that doesn't come with the textbook"). There's usually a scary sign posted somewhere near the photocopier that warns users away from reproducing materials without written permission. In the meantime, students are blithely sampling images and sounds from the Internet without regard for attribution, "confusing access and plagiarism" (Badke, 2007). If teachers avoid the topic, the students incorrectly understand the silence to mean that there are no guidelines.

But there are guidelines, even if they are rarely taught in classrooms. The Copyright Act of 1976, which protects published works, contains a provision on "fair use." It states that the use of copyrighted material "for purposes such as criticism, comment, news reporting, teaching (including multiple copies for classroom use), scholarship, or research is not an infringement of copyright" (Cornell University Law School, 2009). The purpose of this provision in the law is to protect educational use of materials. Legal judgments about whether the use of copyrighted text, images, or audio constitutes fair use are based on four factors:

1. the purpose and character of the use, including whether such use is of a commercial nature or is for nonprofit educational purposes;

2. the nature of the copyrighted work;

3. the amount and substantiality of the portion used in relation to the copyrighted work as a whole; and

4. the effect of the use upon the potential market for or value of the copyrighted work. (Cornell University Law School, 2009)

The language of the law is sufficiently obtuse that most educators either avoid using particular materials altogether or use them and hope they won't get caught. Neither is a particularly useful model for students, who will also need to make choices about using the works of others. Fortunately, a consortium of education and communications experts collaborated to create materials to make all of this easier to understand. In addition, they developed guidelines in 2008 for students and educators to use in determining whether the doctrine of fair use applies to their situations. These guidelines have been endorsed by a number of respected education groups, including the National Council of Teachers of English. The guidelines can be summarized with five basic principles:

■ **Principle 1.** Educators engaged in media literacy can use copyrighted materials to teach students in classrooms and on school websites. These materials should be properly attributed.

■ **Principle 2.** Educators can integrate copyrighted materials into classroom lesson plans, using proper citations for the materials.

■ **Principle 3.** Educators can share these lessons containing copyrighted materials at conferences and professional development events, including through digital means. Copyrighted material should be properly cited.

■ **Principle 4.** Students can use copyrighted material for classroom assignments and educationally related creative work. Students should be taught how to correctly attribute copyrighted material in their work.

■ **Principle 5.** Student work containing copyrighted materials can be shared in educational venues and on educational networks for the purpose of learning. As always, copyrighted materials need to be adequately cited. (Center for Social Media, 2008)

It is important to note that guidelines are not law and that it is the interpretation of law through court cases that clarifies and refines meaning. Case law on fair use suggests that several conditions must apply:

- The *context and situation* of the usage are such that the benefit to society outweighs the cost to the copyright holder.

- The use is *transformative* in that the material is being used in a way that is substantially different from the intent behind its original creation, and the use gives the material *added value*. (Center for Social Media, 2008)

Still unsure? Nearly everyone deeply involved in fair use will tell you that these factors, guidelines, and principles are not cut-and-dry. As case law continues to shape our understanding of fair usage, especially of digital media, what is allowable may change as well. In an effort to support educators in making decisions about fair use, the American Library Association's Office for Information Technology has created a tool to help. Called the Fair Use Evaluator, this website (http://librarycopyright.net/fairuse) allows you to submit a description of the material you are planning to use and the context in which it will be used. You will receive a time-stamped evaluation, useful in case you are challenged by a copyright holder. If your project does not meet the criteria set for fair use, you will be informed of that as well.

So far we've moved from copyright law and its four factors for determining fair use to guidelines developed by a consortium of media educators and legal experts on classroom applications. Case law has further determined and upheld that an educational context and transformative use provide additional strength to the fair use of properly cited copyrighted material. These complex ideas have themselves been transformed into a series of PowerPoint presentations, music videos, and lesson plans designed with teachers and students in mind and available from the Media Education Lab at Temple University (http://mediaeducationlab.com). As always, keep fair use in mind as you correctly attribute these materials for your students. As we have stated throughout this book, teachers' modeling of the concepts they teach is arguably the most powerful tool they have at their disposal.

Digital access is continuing to reform the landscape of copyright protection, and important issues hang in the balance. On the one hand, copyright was established to protect creative endeavors by ensuring that artists could make a living from their work. On the other hand, the limitations placed on copyrights may artificially inhibit intellectual growth. Nonprofit organizations such as Creative Commons are attempting to bridge this divide, with positive results for students and teachers.

Creative Commons

The stated mission of Creative Commons, which was formed in 2001 in San Francisco, is to "increase sharing and improve collaboration" (Creative Commons, n.d.). A leader in the "copyleft" movement, the organization provides copyright licensing at no cost so that the artist or creator can determine which copyrights should apply to his or her given work. Licensees decide whether their work can be used commercially, if the work can be altered or not, and if subsequent users must also agree to share the new work on CC (called "share alike"). Some creators choose a fourth option, designating the work as public domain and thus free of any copyright protection.

The company estimates that over 130 million works are licensed through it, including high-profile projects such as music by Nine Inch Nails (Creative Commons, n.d., History). The photo-sharing website Flickr (www.flickr.com) allows users to add a Creative Commons license to make images available. In June 2009, Wikipedia announced that a Web-based vote of its community came out overwhelmingly in favor of changing its own licensing agreement to a Creative Commons one that requires attribution and share alike.

The organization is not without criticism. Some of the restrictions dictated by copyright law are meant to protect the rights of the copyright holder. Creative Commons has made a few errors in granting licensing for works that did not actually belong to the applicants. One example would be failing to receive permission from all the participants in an image. It is important to note that there have only been a few of these incidents, and the likelihood that Creative Commons material is not correctly vetted is very small.

The copyleft movement has spread to the science community as well. Projects such as the Health Commons Project (www.healthcommons.net) and NeuroCommons (www.neurocommons.org) allow scientists from across the world to trade data and findings. The Personal Genome Project (www .personalgenomes.org) is amassing DNA mapping results from 100,000 volunteers, allowing researchers to utilize the database in order to implement their studies. The concept is that researchers will not have to waste valuable time locating study volunteers, because the database will already exist. Scientists will be able to specify the typology (Asian women with a family history of breast cancer, adult males between the ages of thirty-five and fifty who smoke, and so on) and perform analyses.

While accessing a genetic database does not have direct classroom implications, the notion of analyzing the results of DNA mapping does. Health teacher Althea Lincoln profiled the work of the Personal Genome Project by showing her ninth-grade students a short video clip (PBS, 2008) and then leading a discussion about the possible benefits of the project. She charted the suggested benefits, such as fueling advances in medicine. She then showed the class the profiles of the first ten people who had contributed their genetic samples to the project (www.personalgenomes.org/public). The students viewed the ten volunteers' profiles, which included disclosed medical histories of cancer, depression, and specific syndromes. Ms. Lincoln asked, "Is there a disadvantage to having information like this out there?" The class discussed a few drawbacks but couldn't really come up with any significant ones, so she next had them read an opinion piece published in the student newspaper *The Harvard Crimson* (Meisel, 2007). The article discussed advantages and disadvantages of making such information public and imagined a presidential candidate of the future who is forced to withdraw because his DNA sequence shows that he carries the gene for Huntington's disease. The class debated the pros and cons, and Ms. Lincoln added their points to the chart.

She then invited the students to watch excerpts from the *NOVA* television program titled "Cracking the Code of Life" (Arledge & Cort, 2001). The excerpts focused on genetic diseases like cystic fibrosis and raised questions about the ethics of genetic testing. Afterward, Ms. Lincoln drew the students' attention back to the reading, specifically the section on the need for legal protections so that people won't be denied employment, housing, or insurance because of their genetics. Having built their background knowledge and introduced complexities that defied simple answers, she had all her students go to an online poll and answer four opinion questions about genetic testing and gene sequencing (visit go.solution-tree.com/literacy to find the URL for the poll). The website reported immediate tabulations of the poll results to date. After each question, the students discussed their opinions and insights and compared them against the opinions of others who had taken the poll. "There aren't any clear-cut answers," Ms. Lincoln remarked later, "but I want them to appreciate how advances in science and technology challenge our decision making."

Essential Questions

Ms. Lincoln and her students were considering the elements of decision making as part of a larger exploration of a schoolwide essential question that asked, "If we can, should we?" The purpose of an essential question is to foster inquiry and speculative oral and written discourse that is supported by factual knowledge (Wiggins & McTighe, 2005). As mentioned in chapter 1, essential questions are deliberately crafted to be open ended and should defy simplistic yes/no answers. This is not to say that anything goes and that all responses are equally meritorious—quite the opposite. The best responses to these complex questions are arguments that include elements of logic (*logos*), emotional appeal (*pathos*), and ethics (*ethos*). The teaching of argumentation is consistent with adolescent intellectual development, as young people in this age group begin to take on propositional reasoning—the ability to arrive at solutions, opinions, and understandings.

As you can imagine, the purpose of essential questions is for students to produce, and not just consume, knowledge. In a literacy 2.0 curriculum, students use a host of tools to demonstrate both their understanding of concepts and their facility with the formal academic thought of argumentation. The major project of the term is a formal essay that addresses the essential question through rhetorical writing that uses *logos, pathos,* and *ethos* to support the student's position. In addition, students respond to the question throughout the term using a number of other formats, such as podcasts, songs, and poetry.

During the nine weeks when the entire school explored the essential question "If we can, should we?" teachers organized the curriculum to foreground concepts related to the question. We saw how Ms. Lincoln did this with her health class. In English, tenth-grade teacher Heather Anderson used the dystopian novel *1984* (Orwell, 1949/2003) as a touchstone text for shared readings, teacher modeling, and class discussion. She also gave students a list of books to choose from for their independent reading so that they could extend their knowledge of course concepts such as literary devices while building their understanding of the complexities inherent in the essential question. Among the titles available to students were:

- The graphic novel *Persepolis*, by Marjane Satrapi (2004), which chronicles her adolescence in a repressive regime

- *Nickel and Dimed: On (Not) Getting By in America*, by Barbara Ehrenreich (2001), a nonfiction account of economic challenges faced by workers across the country

- *The Boy in the Striped Pajamas*, by John Boyne (2006), a novel of the Holocaust, told from the perspective of a small boy

- *The Joy Luck Club*, by Amy Tan (1989/2006), a novel that uses flashback to tell the parallel tales of several generations of an American family in San Francisco and China

- *The Curious Incident of the Dog in the Night-Time*, by Mark Haddon (2003), an account of a neighborhood crime as told by a teenager with autism

- *Wringer*, by Jerry Spinelli (2004), an easier read that describes the moral and ethical conflicts felt by a young boy in a small town with a Pigeon Day shoot

- *The Prince*, by Niccolò Machiavelli (1532/2007), a classic guide on decision making in politics and business

As the students read their chosen books, they met regularly with Ms. Anderson and other students to discuss general literary elements like author's craft, as well as specific aspects of the characters they were reading about, such as the tools of reasoning that they used. Each week, the students wrote "literacy letters" to their teacher to summarize where they were in the book thus far and to discuss their reactions and understandings (Frey, Fisher, & Moore, 2009). Here is an excerpt (used with permission) from a letter by Ryan, who was reading *The Curious Incident of the Dog in the Night-Time*:

> Dear Ms. Anderson,
>
> I am reading *The Curious Incident of the Dog in the Night-Time* by Mark Haddon. It is about a boy that has autism that tries to solve the mystery of who killed his neighbor's dog. He is very intelligent and dislikes talking to people. He has a difficulty with socializing, but he knows how to do very complicated math. The book is a book the character is writing, and he runs into another problem involving his mother while trying to solve the mystery.
>
> I have never read a book about autism. I like how the author puts readers into the mind of a child with autism. They can be very smart and just like normal people, but they have a trouble relating to other humans. People look at autistic people differently, just like in the book. The character showed me that they can think just as logically. Whenever he said something or gave an opinion, he gave a logical reason for it, except for his ticks. He doesn't like yellow or brown, but he never tries to justify it, saying he doesn't like yellow or brown. I think obsessive compulsive disorder might explain his odd habits. I also met a person with autism yesterday. He has an obsession with Naruto and Yu Gi Oh cards. He is a little out of touch with reality, but I understand it better now.
>
> Sincerely,
>
> Ryan

Ryan's weekly discussions with Ms. Anderson, both in person and in writing, helped him to discern the manner in which people make decisions and to see how a person's identity and experiences influence those decisions.

Using iMovie and GarageBand, eleventh-grade student Rita created a multimedia piece to address the essential question in a way that was both personal and academic. When her U.S. history class studied immigration, Rita related the content to her own experience. She and her younger siblings were all born in the United States, but her parents and older brother were not, and some members of her family were undocumented. Rita had grown up in a household where *la migra,* the U.S. Immigration and Customs Enforcement, was ever present in their lives. She wrote a poem for her English class that drew on her understanding of poetry as a vehicle for personal expression. She enhanced the poem with an image (from a photograph she had taken) of a window with the blinds drawn in a darkened room and a soundscape that simulated a beating heart, which was available though Creative Commons licensing. The text of her poem follows (used with permission).

If we can, should we?

Time is running out!
They will find me any second.
I wish I could have been crystal clear!

Why are people so lifeless?
Just because I have brown eyes
Doesn't mean I am dangerous!

How many times do I have to hide?
Why do they judge me for how I look?
I just don't understand!
Moms are yelling.
Kids are running.
Fathers are being wounded
And I am hiding in the darkest
room you'll ever see!

And see, everything is back to normal.
But something deep down in my heart says
That will never happen.

Time is running out!
They will find me any second.
I am almost out of breath.
My blood has suddenly stopped.
What should I do?

Josiah, another eleventh-grade student, was inspired by current world events. He turned the essential question into an interrogation of the role of war as a tool for maintaining and destroying order. He was particularly moved by the dilemma facing soldiers who must make a choice to go against all the norms and values they have been taught in order to take a human life. As a young man nearing the age when he would need to register for the draft, Josiah was beginning to question whether he would be capable of making this decision. He researched the laws pertaining to conscientious objectors and read about draft dodgers who fled to Canada during the Vietnam War. For his English class, he read the novel *Slap Your Sides* (Kerr, 2001) about a young Quaker who refuses to serve in World War II. He also watched the documentary *The Conscientious Objector* (Benedict, 2004) about Desmond Doss, who was awarded the Congressional Medal of Honor for his service as a medic in World War II. Josiah learned that Doss refused the deferment he was entitled to and served in battles in the Pacific theater. Using the GarageBand program, Josiah wrote, produced, and recorded an original song titled "If I Can Then Why Can't I?" to portray the paradox of a soldier who was been given the license to shoot to kill but finds that he can't pull the trigger. The text to Josiah's song follows (used with permission).

If I Can Then Why Can't I?

Intro

If I can then why can't I?

My living deed

The decision's mine

I lie still

The pain intervenes

I miss my life the living scene

Verse

Red the color coming from his head

The color soaked the soldier's bed

The privilege given to me

It's the privilege that I weep

Chorus

If it's there then why can't I?

If it's his will to live or die

If it's there then why can't I

If it's his will to live or die

For you

And me

If we can then should we?

Verse

Day to night

I'm losing sight

Of all of this s**t

This is the life

I gave you a choice you chose one way

Now you're gone out of misery

Misery

Chorus

If it's there then why can't I?

If it's his will to live or die

Tonight

If it's there then why can't I?

If it's his will to live or die

For you

And me

If we can then should we

Do no harm?

The learning experiences of Ryan, Rita, Josiah, and others are prime examples of combining the "old" and "new" literacies of a literacy 2.0 curriculum. Students use the more traditional reading, writing, speaking, and listening elements of learning, as well as the tools afforded by technological advancements that allow them to create and share knowledge using sounds, words, and images. The emphasis, as always, is on the verbs.

Chapter Tweets

New Literacies invite students to use the tools of language to create knowledge. The trick for us is to figure out how to do it!

Podcasts allow students to produce information in a format that is readily accessible.

Podcasts also cause students to monitor their conceptual understandings through playback.

Video tools give students the opportunity to combine text and images to produce original works.

Fair use laws and guidelines give educators more latitude than is often believed in accessing materials for classrooms.

Creative Commons seeks to further increase access to images, sounds, and data in order to accelerate the knowledge base.

Essential questions form a foundation for original thinking as students build their frameworks using information from a host of sources.

Chapter 5

Sharing Information: The World Is Your Audience

One of the milestones in our transition to literacy 2.0 teaching came several years ago when a student asked if she could write her book review on Amazon.com rather than on paper. Amber, who had read *Who Will Tell My Brother?* (Carvell, 2002), wanted to share her thoughts about the book with other people who had read it. She really enjoyed the poetic format of the book and at the same time was angry about the mascot issue raised in the story. She wanted to know if this kind of thing happened in other places or if it was "just fiction." She wanted to connect with other readers, and she understood that this relatively new service would allow her to do so. As she said, "Nobody else in class has read it, but somebody out there has, and I wanna talk with them." Despite our concerns about this new venue, we encouraged her to post a comment about the book and promised that we would read her comment and discuss it with her. Were we scared to let her share her developing voice with the whole world? Yes. Did we understand her desire to do so? Of course. And did we learn something along the way? You bet.

Looking back on this experience, we're almost embarrassed to talk about it. Today, students post reviews on hundreds of topics on thousands of websites. Reviews on Amazon.com are rather simplistic compared with the blogs students create today. But that's what 2.0 applications are all about—engagement and collaboration with a significantly wider audience. And that's what we learned from Amber: audience matters.

Audience Matters

Of course, as writing teachers in the 20th century, we taught students to focus on audience (and our predecessors taught students about audience in the 19th century). As Dean (2006) reminds us, audience is one of the teachable aspects of writing. There is even evidence that first-graders can be taught the importance of audience (Wollman-Bonilla, 2001).

One concept we stress when teaching about audience is *language registers*. When speakers or writers have a sophisticated understanding of language registers, they can communicate in a wide variety of settings and with diverse members of society. While language registers are important in most aspects of life, systematic instruction in them is critical for students today. Given that the reader or listener is often not in the physical presence of the author or speaker, a mismatch between the expected register and the observed register can be disastrous. We've all experienced this mismatch when students use slang in the classroom, incorporate texting phrases in their writing (R U sure?), or incorporate fixed language (without attribution) into their work. We use the following definitions of language registers in our teaching:

- **Fixed or frozen**. Fixed speech is reserved for traditions in which the language does not change. Examples of fixed speech include the Pledge of Allegiance, Shakespeare plays, and civil ceremonies such as weddings.

- **Formal**. At the formal level, speech is expected to be presented in complete sentences with specific word usage. Formal language is the standard for work, school, and business and is more often seen in writing than in speaking. However, public speeches and presentations are expected to be delivered in a formal language register.

- **Consultative**. The third level of language, consultative, is formal register used in conversations. Less appropriate for writing, students often use consultative language in their interactions in the classroom.

- **Casual**. This is the language that is used in conversations with friends. In casual speech, word choice is general and conversation is dependent upon non-verbal assists, significant background knowledge, and shared information.

- **Intimate**. This is the language used by very close friends and lovers. Intimate speech is private and requires significant amounts of shared history, knowledge, and experience. (Frey & Fisher, 2006, p. 210)

In addition to learning about language registers, students must learn to consider the audience as they create. We teach them that there are three main audience types:

- *Laypeople* have no special topical information or expertise. They are interested in the human aspect of the writing and want to find things out. Their background knowledge prevents them from understanding writing that is highly technical or filled with jargon. They expect definitions and explanations and appreciate graphics and illustrations of main ideas.

- *Middle people*, also known as "managerial audience members," have some information, and often have an opinion, about the topic. They have varying degrees of background knowledge and expect some analysis of the issue. They are looking for recommendations and added information.

- *Experts* are often the most demanding audience members. They have lots of background knowledge about the topic and expect very accurate information and not general information. They expect the vocabulary to be technical and specialized and look for thoughtful analyses of the issue or topic.

Once students have started thinking about different audiences, we use the RAFT writing prompt developed by Santa and Havens (1995). This prompt focuses students, as writers, on Role, Audience, Format, and Topic. A sample RAFT writing prompt might be:

Role: Thomas Jefferson

Audience: Barack Obama

Format: Letter of advice

Topic: Explaining my quote "A democracy is nothing more than mob rule, where fifty-one percent of the people may take away the rights of the other forty-nine."

In identifying the audience, we've communicated to students that the letter should be somewhat formal. It is for the president of the United States, after all.

In reality, of course, the audience for the RAFT assignment is limited to the teacher and the other students. The prompt provides students with a *practice* audience but not an *authentic* audience. With the Internet, this situation changes dramatically, as people all over the world can see and comment on whatever is posted. And that's what we really need to teach students—that there is an audience and the audience is listening or reading or watching. Moreover, quite frankly, with the anonymity the Internet provides, the audience isn't always very nice. If you doubt that, look at the posts on a YouTube page; they can be brutal. We know that the Internet did not create rude audience members. We're reminded of the British Parliament debates we've seen on TV and the hecklers we've seen at professional conferences. But the Internet expands the number of people who can serve as an audience, for better or worse. And our students are putting their ideas and work out there, so we have to guide them along the way. The place we'll start is with blogs.

"*My* Words Are Everywhere": Blogging Creates an Audience

When Tyler showed us his blog and said, "*My* words are everywhere," we realized how powerful blogging had become. Tyler has something to say and wants to say it to anyone who will listen. He likes the reactions he gets, and those reactions shape his future blog entries. It becomes a cycle in which the writer (blogger) adds new content, reads, reflects, and then writes some more. And unlike literacy 1.0 efforts, writing in this way provides students with direct experiences in which they learn that there is no one "writing process" but rather a number of processes that writers use based on audience, purpose, format, and topic (Fisher & Frey, 2007b).

Parenthetically, blogs aren't just for teenagers who want to describe everything that happens in their lives. By now, we are all familiar with Julie Powell's blog about her attempt to master the art of French cooking (Powell, 2002). Unlike most blogs, hers became a best-selling book (Powell, 2005) and then a major motion picture. Blogs are becoming a staple of the writerly life in the 21st century.

Thankfully, blogs aren't hard to create. For example, WordPress is free blogging software that just about anyone can use after investing fifteen minutes' time becoming familiar with it (http://wordpress.org). For those of us who need to read a book to figure out how to blog, there is a great resource called *Building a WordPress Blog People Want to Read* (McNulty, 2009). There are also blogging services available for schools and classrooms, such as ePals (www.epals .com) and Class Blogmeister (http://classblogmeister.com). One of our colleagues has his students on ePals weekly, writing to other students all over the world. And guess what they mostly blog about? Yes, school and schoolwork!

Blogs are showing up in educational circles in a wide array of forms. For example, author Daniel Waters (2008) created a character in his book *Generation Dead* who blogs "as a way to build a community of support for his fellow undead" (Harris, 2009, p. 16). Interestingly, the blog continues as readers contribute and the character adds information not in the book (http://mysocalledundeath.blogspot.com). There's a math teacher who blogs (http://blog.mrmeyer.com), and there are students blogging in their health classes (Burke & Oomen-Early, 2008). And of course, there are English teachers who use blogs to focus on writing (Bass, 2009).

In our own school, we've witnessed the power of blogs in teaching and learning. For their U.S. history class, students complete fieldwork both during the school day and as part of their extended learning beyond school hours. They visit sites such as the Museum of Tolerance, spend the day on an aircraft carrier, interview people in the community, search for primary source

documents on the Internet, walk through parts of San Diego that have historical significance (especially in relation to World War II), and so on. An important aspect of their fieldwork is documenting their experiences using digital
cameras or their phones. (They understand the sensitive nature of some of
the information and are aware of restricted areas where they cannot take pictures.) They each post the images they find and blog about their experiences
learning history.

For example, Jessie took a photo with a World War II prisoner of war who
had just presented his story in connection with an exhibition. In her blog,
Jessie wrote:

> I didn't know that so many Americans were captured and had to survive
> in POW camps. Someone had to run the POW camps. They had to watch
> as other humans tried to live. It just makes me think about the impact of
> war on people, not just the soldiers. The people who worked at the POW
> camps had to go home to their families every night and probably didn't
> want to talk about their day at work. At least the workers didn't torture the
> POWs and gave them food and water to live. But the conditions weren't
> good. Meeting a real POW made the war even more real for me than the
> book I'm reading.

Jessie had been reading the book *American POWs of World War II: Forgotten
Men Tell Their Stories* (Bird, 1992). Combining what she learned from the book
with her direct experiences and the opportunity to blog about them ensured
that she had a much deeper understanding of this time in history.

To expand their Spanish language learning opportunities, some of our students travel to Mexico in the summer and live with host families and take
classes. A group of these students created a blog to record their experiences
and share them with their families and their teachers. In one entry, they took
a picture in front of a large statue and wrote, "Can you name this famous man
from Mexican history?" Another entry was about the cooking class they took.
One of the students posted several pictures and wrote, "Yesterday we had a
cooking class. We made fish tacos. They were so great we could start our own
taco stand! Today's pictures are from the cooking class. School is challenging
us mentally and physically. Hay mucho trabajo." On the second-to-last day of
class in Mexico, one of the students wrote, "Yesterday in school we received
a play script to memorize and perform on Friday. We also practiced more
vocabulary related to medical professions. After school we went to a movie
(in English) out at the 'Macro Plaza' where we ate Burger King, Subway, and
Thrifty ice cream."

These blog entries from the language immersion in Mexico remind us that
students in the 21st century want to write and share their experiences with
a wider audience, even when they don't have to. The students who went to

Mexico knew that their readers included their families, peers, friends, and teachers, and they wrote appropriately for this diverse audience.

Our final example comes from a friend and colleague who teaches math. As part of her personal literacy 2.0 efforts, she decided to create a blog about her math class. She took a picture or two of the dry-erase board each day with her iPhone, posted the photos on her blog, and then wrote about her experiences. Some of the entries focused on concepts she was teaching, and others focused on the successes she observed in students. Sometimes, she expressed frustration with her inability to explain a concept in a way that resulted in student learning. The primary audience for her blog was her students. It was an amazing experience for us to see students responding to her postings, affirming her teaching, recognizing the usefulness of the added explanations, and reassuring her that she did make the content understandable. Nearly every student post included the words THANK YOU, which strengthened the bond between teacher and learners.

As we said before, blogs aren't hard to create. Teaching students about audience and how to interact in this environment is much harder. As we have noted throughout this book, we don't need to focus on the specific tools (in this case blogs), because they will change. Rather, we should focus on the function these tools serve—in this case, sharing one's ideas with the world. We have found the National Public Radio Community Discussion Rules to be particularly helpful in this regard. Lessons on each of the following topics are helpful not only for teaching students about blogs but for creating norms of communication for students in the 21st century:

- If you can't be polite, don't say it.
- Don't use obscenities—even if the word in question is often used in conversation.
- Anything you post should be your own work.
- Please stay on topic.
- Rambling is the kiss of death.
- Please respect people's privacy.
- Feel free to share your ideas and experiences about religion, politics and relevant products or services you've discovered. (National Public Radio, n.d.)

Microblogs: Tweeting the World

Some newer communication formats are being shaped by the users themselves. Microblogs such as Twitter and Tumblr are a format for providing very brief (usually limited to 140 characters) multimedia blogs. Users can send text, audio, or video files to a group of subscribers using a smartphone or computer.

Social networking sites such as Facebook feature a version of microblogging known as the status update. As noted several times throughout this book, the specific tools will continue to change at a rapid rate; our interest is in considering the ways in which these tools function within literacy practices.

Adopting a function-oriented, rather than tools-oriented, perspective on technology allows us to focus on our long-term goals as educators. We couldn't help but notice that this same belief is shared by others, even if it is not labeled as such. A friend of ours forwarded an article by Laura Doggett, director of e-learning at a secondary school in the United Kingdom. In "Nine Great Reasons Why Teachers Should Use Twitter," Doggett (2009) provides compelling evidence for the use of a new technology, all based on its functions:

1. **Together we're better.** Twitter can be like a virtual staffroom where teachers can access in seconds a stream of links, ideas, opinions, and resources from a hand-picked selection of global professionals.

2. **Global or local: you choose.** With Twitter, educators can actively compare what's happening in their schools with others on different continents. GPS-enabled devices and the advanced web search facility allow searches that tell you what people are tweeting within a certain distance of a location, so if the other side of the world isn't your bag, you can stick with your own patch.

3. **Self-awareness and reflective practice.** Excellent teachers reflect on what they are doing in their schools and look at what is going well in order to maintain and develop it, and what needs improvement in order to make it better. Teachers on Twitter share these reflections and both support and challenge each other.

4. **Ideas workshop and sounding board.** Twitter is a great medium for sharing ideas and getting instant feedback. You can gather a range of opinions and constructive criticism within minutes, which can help enormously, whether you are planning a learning experience, writing a policy, or putting a job application together.

5. **Newsroom and innovation showcase.** Twitter helps you stay up-to-date on news and current affairs, as well as on the latest developments in areas of interest like school leadership and technology.

6. **Professional development and critical friends.** One of the best things about training days is the break-out time between sessions, when teachers can get together to talk about what they are working on or struggling with. Twitter enables users to have that kind of powerful networking capacity with them all the time. It's just a matter of finding the right people to follow.

7. **Quality-assured searching.** Trust the people you follow. Hone and develop the list of people whose insights you value. Once your Twitter network grows past a critical mass, you can ask them detailed questions and get higher-quality information back than a Google search would generally provide.

8. **Communicate, communicate, communicate.** Expressing yourself in 140 characters is a great discipline. I have become better at saying what needs to be said in my professional communications with less waffle and padding (even without txtspk).

9. **Getting with the times has never been so easy!** Twitter is anything but complicated! You simply visit Twitter.com and create your account. A little light searching using key words for your areas of interest will soon yield a list of interesting people to follow. There are plenty of Web sites offering advice on getting started and how to avoid a few common beginners' *faux pas.* Your biggest challenge is likely to be getting twitter.com unblocked on your school network if your main usage will be at school. (Doggett, 2009. Used with permission.)

Focusing on these functions and helping students learn to communicate with the world through microblogs draws on literacy 1.0 skills while building literacy 2.0 knowledge and expertise.

"I Got 159 Hits Yesterday": Representing Yourself via the Web

How many websites are there, and does the world need another one? Interesting questions, but not ones that are really on the minds of most students. (For those of you who love a number, in March 2010 there were more than 115 million active websites [DomainTools, 2010]). If students have something to say and want a place to organize that information, they regard a website as a perfect container. Student-generated webpages are becoming increasingly common. Yes, of course students go to numerous webpages every day, including the top hits such as Google, MySpace, and Facebook, as well as webpages that provide them with specific information. But for many students, that's too Web 1.0. They want to have their own website and figure out how to direct traffic to it. And that's the context for the quote from Paula that appears in the heading to this section. After updating her webpage, she got 159 hits and couldn't wait to tell us about it.

As we have said before, this book is less about the specific tools and more about the functions related to literacy 2.0. Websites are one of the ways that students engage in sharing, but there are others. And websites are probably the most complicated topic we'll address in this book. As you've no doubt noticed, this isn't a technical book. There are great resources for building webpages, especially if you want to learn how to write in code (also known as html). For our purposes, there are a number of resources that teachers and students can use to create a Web presence.

Our students have experience with iWeb (which is part of the iLife package) and DreamWeaver. There are also free, open-source software tools for

creating webpages. The Open Source Web Design site (www.oswd.org) provides free Web design templates. Ninth-grade media arts teacher Mr. Benson
uses a high school Web design and development curriculum that is available
through the AccessIT program at the University of Washington (2005–2008).
Lessons cover topics such as color theory and layout of information, managing
a website, creating tags to drive traffic, and linking to other websites.

Of course, students will also need a hosting service and some technical
assistance to launch their pages. For this, the teacher will probably need to
access the school technology coordinator. But students aren't ready to launch
webpages just because they want to. In addition to the technical information
they'll need to design their Web presence, they need to consider the audience
and how their page will attract readers. As Ohler (2009) notes, "effective blog
or webpage writing requires using visually differentiated text" (p. 11). We have
adopted his formatting conventions, which he calls the 6 Bs.

- Bullets—Readers of webpages like to have lists that they can manage,
  and a list of bulleted topics meets this need. The list format also requires
  that the writer create concise topical sentences that can be linked to
  additional information deeper into the webpage.

- Boldface—Given that not every word on a webpage is equally important, some of the key words should be presented in boldface type. This
  allows the reader to scan the page and get a sense of the key ideas and
  topics that are addressed.

- Breaks—Long strings of text are a turn-off to most visitors to webpages.
  They expect breaks in the text and links to additional information.

- Boxes—Graphs, charts, and diagrams (the material set off in boxes)
  help readers find information, use information, and remember information. Webpages shouldn't be lists of running text with hyperlinks,
  but rather the text should be organized into a structure that works for
  the reader and should be presented in a way that provides visual organization. We're all familiar with graphic organizers and their power in
  helping students process information. It's the same idea. Graphic organizers, what Ohler summarizes as "boxes," help the reader synthesize
  and summarize content.

- Beyond black and white—Webpages aren't supposed to be printed and
  experienced offline. In contrast with creating print materials, it doesn't
  cost more to use color in webpage design, and it is visually more appeal-
  ing to most of us. Using color and having a color scheme help the reader
  navigate the site and allow the writer to highlight specific aspects of
  content. Of course, we've all seen webpages where color was not coor-
  dinated, and the result is an immediate turn-off.

- Beginnings—Given the astounding number of choices webpage readers have, the opening content is critical to maintaining interest. The introduction has to be engaging and has to entice the reader to want more. Also, most webpage readers don't want to scroll down the page, but rather they want to click through pages. We all have experience with this. If there are pages and pages that we have to scroll through, we're very likely to leave that site and find another that is more consistent with our expectations and more conducive to our learning.

Another element of webpage design that should be taken into account is accessibility for people with physical disabilities. Access to instructional materials was legislated in 2006 and has been aligned with the principles of Universal Design for Learning, an approach to curriculum and instruction that seeks to minimize accessibility problems for students.

Using the tools offered by Google Sites (http://sites.google.com), students in our school's media arts class created websites related to the essential question "Does age matter?" As we have discussed before, our curriculum is organized around essential questions that change every year. This approach gives both teachers and students an opportunity to dig deeply into content and keeps us all fresh. But back to creating websites. Students learned to use design tools and manipulated content from their other classes to develop a resource for their peers. The assignment required them to discuss both sides of the question: age does and does not matter.

As part of her investigation of the essential question, Lapresha read a series of books by Dave Pelzer, starting with *A Child Called It* (1993). When her English class was assigned to write "I am" poems, Lapresha wrote this one about Dave (used with permission):

I Am Dave Pelzer

I am from an abusive family, from an alcoholic mother and dark basement

I am from the 1960's of "Baby Boomers"

From where my mother made me drink ammonia at age 10

I am from an alcoholic environment and no friends

From "you dumbass" and beating on little kids

I am from a fireman

I am from the legacy of drinking until you are naked

From tall and slender and grey or blue eyes and crying until my eyes had no water left in them

I am from a place of no hope or no thought of survival

Lapresha posted this poem on her website. When the poem page launched, very sad background music played. Lapresha said, "I wanted to make it sound like I felt when I read the book." Several of her peers added comments about the poem on her webpage, so Lapresha decided to add a video clip of herself talking about the book and how she felt about it. She also added links to other resources, including the child abuse hotline and a survivor group. Sharing her thinking with the world gave her an opportunity to continue reading and writing. It also provided her with motivation to go beyond the assigned task and make the project her own. We couldn't say it any better than Lapresha, who said, "People are reading what I wrote and asking me about it. I feel like a real author. I don't wanna put junk out there because they expect better from me."

"She Made It Even Better": Using Collaborative Tools

The collaborative tools that started to appear at the end of the 20th century have become common in many schools. The advent of cloud computing—whereby storage of information is Web-based rather than restricted to local hardware, such as a computer hard drive or server—has made collaborative efforts much more feasible. (We love vocabulary: the term *cloud computing* comes from the general shape of network diagrams, which often resemble clouds [Scanlon & Wieners, 1999].) Before this development, it was difficult to manage the collaborative creation of documents and presentations, because the electronic transfer of the materials got in the way. We know that documents in our own writing projects often got tangled up as we traded them back and forth, and we would inadvertently wind up working on earlier, outdated versions.

One of the best-known collaborative systems relies on wiki software to manage websites. The most famous application of this is Wikipedia, which allows a large number of contributors to continually edit one another's work. Wikis can be truly public like Wikipedia, or they can be controlled to limit access. Wikis such as Google Docs and Wikispaces, a nonprofit that offers free wikis for classroom use, are especially helpful. Students can be enrolled in small-group wikis so that the materials they are developing together are seen only by the members of the group.

For instance, English teacher Matt Growe uses wikis in his class whenever students are developing research reports on assigned topics. The wiki allows the members of the group to write on a single document and saves them the trouble of having to email versions to one another. This not only streamlines the work process for his students but also makes it possible for Mr. Growe to check in on their progress. He includes himself as a member of every wiki, allowing him access to the documents in progress. He can check them anytime and can add comments, make suggestions, and even provide a level of editing long before the assignment is completed. "It makes my assessment more for-mative, rather than summative," he commented. "If a group is going off in the wrong direction early in the research process, I can guide them back, when it really matters." The main benefit, however, is that students can see what their group members are contributing. "She made it even better!" one student exclaimed after reading the contributions from another group member. "I didn't even think to add that section on the author's biography, but she did."

Wikis are especially useful for creating documents, but they are limited to text-based works. A favorite tool is VoiceThread (www.voicethread.com), a free collaborative system that allows for video streaming and annotation by observers. Students can create presentations together using still images and audio or text-based commentary. In addition, viewers can post their own com-ments and questions, in either audio, video, or text form, as they watch the presentation online. In our practice, we have found VoiceThread to be particu-larly valuable for enabling students to check their own presentation styles, as they can record, play back, delete, and re-record until they are satisfied with the result. The site also offers a number of wikis established by educators on how they use VoiceThread in their classrooms.

An example of a VoiceThread that reached a global audience is "Many Voices on Darfur," a project aimed at raising awareness about the genocide in that region (Darth Tater, 2008). Over 250,000 young people from around the world participated, and many contributed to the VoiceThread established for the project. The audience viewed seven political cartoons and engaged in debate and discussion about both the artists' messages and the complexities of political, humanitarian, and military responses.

"Being Watched Now": Representing Yourself in Moving Images

Of the late 20th century revolutions on the Internet, YouTube has to be one of the biggest. Unlike any other time in history, today everyone can self-broadcast. We've already talked about creating videos, so we won't repeat that here. It is well known that teachers often show YouTube videos in class (Trier, 2007). To our thinking, YouTube is among the greatest free resources ever created for teachers. Of course, we know that YouTube is blocked in most schools. But teachers can download the videos they want to show using a simple website: www.keepvid.com. All you have to do is insert the URL from YouTube into the appropriate line on KeepVid and click the download button. But YouTube can be used for more than showing students videos. This chapter is about students sharing information with the world, and YouTube is a great resource for doing exactly that. In this section, we'll give three examples of students creating videos, posting those videos for the world, and learning from the reactions to them. In their biology class, students borrowed plastic models of different organs or structures of the human body from their teacher. Either at school after hours or at home, they recorded themselves with the plastic model, naming all of the parts. They loaded the videos into YouTube for their teacher and peers to review. For example, Jeffrey borrowed the plastic model of the brain and identified each of the lobes, several of the major landmarks (such as the *lateral sulcus* and *supermarginal gyrus*), and a number of areas associated with specific functions (such as primary visual cortex, Broca's area, and the sensory and motor strips). Fully aware that he'd done his best, he expected feedback from his teachers and peers in the form of comments on YouTube. One of the comments read, "You're really fast at this, you know a lot about the brain already. Well done!" Another person wrote, "Can you also show where Wernicke's area is?" and another wrote, "You forgot to include the location of the angular gyrus which is part of the language circuit." As was planned, Jeffrey removed his first-attempt video and re-recorded it to address the feedback he received. The result was that Jeffrey developed much better understanding of neuroanatomy (and of all the other anatomy and physiology lessons his class completed).

In their English class, students were learning about the concept of back-story. Of course, every reader knows that there are things that the author doesn't directly tell the reader, but the students hadn't really considered the fact that authors have a very specific backstory in mind as they write. As part of the investigation about backstory, students watched a video called "Your Three Words." There have been several versions of this on YouTube, but the idea was that people could submit videos with only three words and any images they wanted. We remember one video of a paramedic who is taking off in a helicopter and turns over his gloved hand, on which he has written, "Saved a life."

For each of the first few examples on this video, the teacher modeled her thinking about the backstory. She thought aloud about the context and what the author might be saying. Then students worked in groups to analyze different aspects of the video and present their backstories to the rest of the class. As a culminating project, the class produced their own version of this video, with each member of the class contributing three words and a video image. In the process, they wrote their own backstories. As Daniel said, "I used to just write whatever was on my mind. Now I plot it out more. I think about the backstory and the things I don't want to directly tell the reader." The result of this exploration was an incredible level of understanding about the importance of back-stories and much better writing on the part of students. In other words, the literacy 2.0 efforts of this teacher also improved her students' literacy 1.0 skills.

Our final example comes from the health class. As most educators know, H1N1 (formerly known as "swine flu") became a great concern in 2009. The health teacher wanted to be sure that students and their families had a reasonable understanding of the disease, including how it was transmitted, appropriate infection prevention measures, and what to do when an infection occurred. Students in this class were given choices of which aspect of H1N1 to focus on and how to present the information. Some students created brochures that were copied and distributed in the community while others developed PowerPoint presentations that were used during back-to-school sessions. Members of one group created a billboard and asked the county health department if they could post it in the community. And some students created informational videos that were posted on YouTube.

One of these student videos focuses on the fear that some people have regarding H1N1. The video starts with a scene that looks like a ghost town (it's really a Lego creation) and asks the question, "Is this what you expect from H1N1?" Then a student comes on screen and says, "If so, you're not alone. People are scared. But we can protect ourselves. Let's learn how." The video then reviews some of the prevention measures recommended by the Centers for Disease Control, such as handwashing and keeping surfaces clean.

The students were very proud of the creations and reported that they felt like they were contributing to the well-being of the community. As one of them said, "I had to teach my mom about this. She was scared to go out, but I showed her our video about safety." Again, when there is an authentic audience and one that provides feedback, students produce incredible work.

"Have You Seen It Yet?" Representing Yourself Through the Works of Others

One of the ways that students represent themselves is through the work of others. They borrow pieces of songs, images, texts, videos, and webpages to create a unique version that demonstrates their thinking and understanding. While some people think it's stealing, students think of this practice as "sampling" and regard the new work as their own creation, something that represents their intellectual contribution. As we have discussed in previous chapters, part of our responsibility as literacy 2.0 educators is to ensure that students understand copyright, plagiarism, fair use, and how to attribute sources. When they do, and they borrow appropriately from other sources, the results are impressive.

Mashups

One of the ways that students can represent themselves through the work of others is through something called a mashup. There are video mashups, song mashups, and Web mashups. Essentially, as Wikipedia notes, a mashup is a combination of multiple sources that usually have no relevance to one another.

The key is that the producer sees a relationship where one did not exist before. Mashups are often humorous, such as "Must Love Jaws," a combination of the romantic comedy *Must Love Dogs* and the classic thriller *Jaws* in which music cues and humorous scenes turn visual source material from *Jaws* into a story about a man who falls in love with a shark. There was even an award for the best Web mashup (http://mashupawards.com).

The best source that we have found for teaching students about mashups is an online tutorial created by members of the library staff at the University of Pennsylvania (2008). The steps they provide are very clear and detailed, and the instructions remind students about permissions and rights issues.

Our students love to put together these demonstrations of their knowledge. Eleventh-grader Edith created a mashup in response to the essential question we have mentioned several times, "Does age matter?" She used her background knowledge of world history and U.S. history to pose the question "Does age matter in a time of war?" Edith used a haunting melody and overlaid still images of child soldiers in Africa and young members of the Zapatista Army of National Liberation in the Mexican state Chiapas, all of whom had scarves covering their faces to disguise their identities. After inserting text asking, "Can it be poverty?" she showed pictures from conflicts around the world, including Darfur, Iraq, and the Congo. She situated her question historically by using images from the Spanish-American War and World Wars I and II: the explosion of the *USS Maine,* doughboys engaged in trench warfare, the cover of the book *Triumph and Tragedy* by Winston Churchill, and political cartoons from the 1940s questioning the high cost of human lives. Edith offered a dictionary definition of *corruption,* showed world leaders from across the globe, and focused on Fidel Castro's and Che Guevara's impact on Cuba. She closed the video with disturbing images of mothers from around the world grieving for their dying children. All of this in four minutes. Her accompanying essay explored these ideas in more detail, but it was her use of music, words, and images in this mashup that had a lingering effect on the viewers in her school.

Mashups continue to evolve as more forms of media become available to the public. Machinima (rhymes with "cinema") uses moving images from films and video games, as well as music and texts. An example from popular culture is a machinima that was submitted to a contest sponsored by recording artists Duran Duran to promote a new song. It was shot in Second Life (more about that in the next chapter) and incorporates Duran Duran videos of earlier songs (Silenticeriver, 2008). Machinima is in its early stages of educational application but is being embraced by higher education fields such as communication, media studies, animation, and film. Because machinima is typically created using a virtual world, future applications may be found in history and anthropology, as well as in the physical sciences, especially in the study of geological and climate phenomena.

On Their Own Time

In our 20th century teaching lives that focused on literacy 1.0, students drew a line between school literacy and the use of reading, writing, speaking, and listening beyond the school day. That's no longer the case. Literacy educators such as Hinchman, Alvermann, Boyd, Brozo, and Vacca (2003) remind us that literacy should not be limited to events that occur between the school bells. Instead, "literacy walks (or runs) right off the page, into the street, the theater, or the community" (Lunsford, 2009, p. 397). And that's the impact that our focus on literacy 2.0 has had. Students engage in literacy tasks in a wide variety of environments, both inside and outside of school. Along the way, they become increasingly skilled at negotiating the terrain and making adjustments based on their purpose and audience. We can't think of a better example than a posting that Lapresha made on her Facebook page on the last day of school (used by permission). She wrote:

As It Comes to an End

As I sit here in class,

I observe my friends

And I look forward to the year

Coming to an end.

It's gonna be sad

To say good-bye.

I'll miss everyone.

I know I will cry.

I remember the day

When I came back

To be with friends

And get on the right track.

We had so many moments;

Some bad, most great.

I'll always remember the love

And erase the hate.

I don't wanna say good-bye

To all my friends.

I don't want this year

To come to an end.

Chapter Tweets

Writers have always valued audience. Literacy 2.0 gives new and authentic meaning to the word.

The better the command of language registers, the better a student will be in addressing his or her audience accurately.

Blogs broaden the audience of young writers. Understanding a community's guidelines about blogs can help ensure publication.

Take student journals online by hosting blogs about school experiences. It adds meaning when students know others will read it.

Student-created websites are more formal than blogs and allow students to develop knowledge more comprehensively.

Don't forget Universal Design for Learning principles when teaching about Web design. It's another aspect of keeping the audience in mind.

Collaborative tools like wikis have simplified group work. Many wiki applications allow for limited audiences.

Students create moving images to represent themselves and their understanding of content. A picture can be worth 1000 words.

Mashups and machinimas are created to synthesize knowledge by showing relationships between concepts. Isn't that the point of learning?

Chapter 6

Present Tense and Future Tensions

Planning is bringing the future into the present so you can do something about it now.

—Alan Lakein

This quote by a time management author was originally written for a business audience but is equally applicable to 21st century learning. An ongoing challenge in any field is to address the problems of the present without sacrificing all the energies needed for planning the work of tomorrow. However, the unknown nature of the future can create a level of discomfort that causes even the best of us to retreat to the known qualities of today. Conversely, a view that is strictly fixed on the horizon places one at risk of tripping over the present. Educators must keep apprised of both present and future developments in order to address today's concerns in anticipation of tomorrow's challenges.

Present Tense

Talk to most teachers, administrators, curriculum coordinators, or technology specialists about 21st century skills, and the issue of access is likely to come up within two minutes. Some will speak of the digital divide that exists between rich and poor and the impediments that occur when learners lack computers or Internet access at home. Others will speak of the expense of retrofitting aging school buildings for digital access and the challenges of multiple platforms and the attendant incompatibility issues. Still others will cite the financial burdens faced by schools already stretched to the limit.

All of these concerns come down to issues of access. Do students have access to the tools they need in order to learn about the functions that under-lie literacy processes? Do teachers have access to the tools they need in order to offer curriculum and instruction that foster 21st century and literacy 2.0 learning for their students? And do administrators and parents have access to policies and procedures that do not unnecessarily inhibit learning?

Student Access and the Changing Shape of the Digital Divide

When originally described in the popular media in the late 1990s, the digi-tal divide—that is, the gap that exists between those who have access to tech-nology and those who do not, was primarily associated with hardware. Schools ramped up the purchase of desktops and laptops, and communities around the country installed hardware in places like libraries in order to eliminate ownership as a criterion for access. By the turn of this century, the digital divide changed and was measured in terms of access to the Internet. Again, the advent of wireless communications and smartphone technologies is begin-ning to narrow this divide as well, at least in the developed world. Schools have become more responsive to the needs of students who may not have Internet access at home, making computers available long before the school day begins and across the day into early evening.

While issues of access to hardware and broadband persist, they are decreas-ing as more supports are created within a community. The digital divide now pertains to disparities in the ability to utilize information and communication technologies in order to meet one's needs. Author Mark Warschauer notes that in too many places, we settle for "the most basic kind of computer lit-eracy instruction, where students learn little more than how to make, save, and access documents," when instead we should "help learners enter new com-munities and cultures, tackle meaningful problems, and address situations of social inequity" (2003, p. 125). He goes on to say that the inability to find, use, and create information leads to social exclusions that marginalize people eco-nomically and legislatively. In addition, as we noted in chapter 3, the inability to evaluate information puts people at risk for exploitation and further dis-tances them from civic engagement in their communities.

The implications for the classroom are voiced throughout this book. It is imperative that all students, and especially those who arrive at our schools with economic and language proficiency disadvantages, be immersed in a literacy-rich learning environment that challenges them in new ways to find and use information and produce and share knowledge. Realizing this vision may require educators to develop creative ways of ensuring that students have access to the hardware and broadband they need to practice literacy 2.0 func-tions, including opening the doors beyond the traditional school day and year.

On a positive note, students and teachers are benefiting from the growing availability of digital textbooks. This phenomenon echoes the rise of digital trade books, which have been available for several years on a variety of e-readers and smartphones. In the summer of 2009, the California Department of Education approved ten open-source digital textbooks for use in high school math and science classes. These digital textbooks make it easy for teachers to customize their instruction, deciding in what order and how thoroughly they will cover the chapters. The most commonly cited benefits of switching to digital textbooks are financial, with estimated savings to schools ranging in the millions of dollars. A concern related to this positive development is that the need for specialized hardware will once again create a divide. Some high schools are making digital sections of courses available to students who own laptops, which can skew class composition along economic lines.

Open sourcing of texts and software is rapidly shaping access to information and service. The goal of open-source developers is to produce reliable software with the contribution of the community, at little to no cost to the end user. Of course, although the software itself may be free or inexpensive, this is not to say that it comes with no additional costs or that it works perfectly for every issue. One must keep in mind that professional development and procedures for change management still need to be carried out accordingly. Schools will incur expenses in purchasing hardware to host the software, such as e-readers, although tailoring the hardware to meet software requirements could be inexpensive if handled in-house. Not everything has a clean-cut solution, but knowing that there are possibilities available and being willing to do some research are two important steps in solving an issue.

Teacher Access to Teaching Tools

A persistent problem for teachers and the technology staff members who support them is the incompatibility of software and hardware products. Nearly all are produced to work on a specific platform (most commonly Mac and PC hardware, and Microsoft software.) Invariably, teachers get excited about a new product, only to learn that it will not work with their system. However, ICT (information and communications technology) managers and technicians have become specialists in making it all work. While it is true that technology doesn't always work the way we expect it to, there is hope. Using the approach of "a goal and an open mind," most issues can be resolved. For example, a teacher at our school needed to run a specific software program for his instruction. The issue was that the teacher was using a Macintosh computer, and the software was compatible only with a Windows operating system. Instead of giving up here or requesting the purchase of another laptop to meet the compatibility requirements, we problem solved using a strengths-based approach.

Since the teacher had an Intel-based MacBook, Alex knew this meant that it would be possible to run a Windows program virtually.

Virtualization consists of three components: the host (in this case the MacBook), the guest operating system (in this case Windows), and finally the virtualization application. This technology allows us to run two or more machines at the same time off of a single machine's physical resources. Without incurring any costs, Alex was able to use an open-source virtualization program, VirtualBox by Sun Microsystems, and the existing Windows XP licensing and media. This allowed the teacher to run Windows on his MacBook and thus to install the class-specific software.

This is only one example of using what's available. It is also an example of why technical knowledge alone won't solve problems. Finding, analyzing, and using information must be part of the equation. Alex had to do quite a bit of Web-based research. He checked blogs he trusts to read questions and answers from other school-based ICT personnel and relied on an RSS news feed he subscribes to as a means for keeping current with the latest innovations. Knowing that the list of software solutions offered by open-source initiatives grows continuously, Alex uses StumbleUpon, the social bookmarking service described in chapter 2 that offers a personalized recommendation engine, allowing him to learn about webpages that could be of interest to him.

Making sure that teachers have access to the tools they need is certainly an ongoing concern, but it is important to remember that it is a shared one. And the good news is that shared concerns can be solved much more rapidly when people are able to trade information freely. This is certainly the underlying philosophy behind projects such as Creative Commons, profiled in chapter 4, the Internet Archive, discussed later in this chapter, and open-source digital textbooks. The continuing democratization of knowledge is providing access to information much more rapidly.

Policies and Procedures That Reflect Literacy 2.0

A persistent challenge in moving to literacy 2.0 is aligning policies and procedures with the changing classroom instructional practices and curricular innovations. We have stated that we come down on the side of teaching students to use their technologies in a courteous fashion, which is certainly an indicator of the awareness of audience. In addition, policies and procedures need to reflect the functions that they are used for. Districts need policies on storage, for example, to protect servers and other infrastructure. Other policies should deal with how students share information, with an eye toward concerns about cyberbullying. If students are to collaborate in their learning, then policies need to be in place regarding access to equipment and the Internet. No student should be excluded from a group because the other group members find it too difficult to communicate with him or her because of lack of access. If it is a given that students need to search, listen, and view, then it is imperative to have procedures for accommodating these activities safely and for ensuring that no student jeopardizes Internet access for others.

We acknowledge that it is tempting to simply ban a host of tools and practices, but prohibitions have rarely worked. While it may be easy to make a rule that says, "No cell phones allowed," the cost in time and effort for the vice principal who has a drawer full of the devices is a high one. Her expertise is being wasted on enforcing a misguided rule. A blanket policy that blocks student access to social networking sites misses the intent of the services provided—to communicate. A more prudent approach would be to allow access during specific hours, such as at lunchtime and before and after school. Around the country we see evidence of these rigid policies changing as educators have come to appreciate how literacy functions interact with new tools. And keep in mind that at one time chalkboards were demonized as a tool that would make teachers lazy.

"Not in This School You Don't"

In most middle and high schools, students are told to "power down" their technology when they arrive on campus. As they do so, students also power down a major way they access information and think. Gone are the days when students looked up words in a paper dictionary; their natural inclination today is to Google anything they want to know. But the power-down policy prevents them from doing so and, in effect, asks students to turn off parts of their brain. Perhaps even worse than creating missed learning opportunities, the power-down policy encourages students to sneak around and break rules. In one school we recently visited, there were signs in every hallway that read, "If we see it, you lose it!" This didn't stop students from accessing their technology. Instead, we saw students stealthily using their handheld devices under the table to send messages and access information. When asked about this, one of the students said, "I just make sure she [pointing to the teacher] never sees it."

In contrast, in some schools, teachers have focused on the use of technology as a learning tool and regularly invite students to power up. Consider a high school history class we observed. As we entered, the teacher was reading aloud from a textbook. As part of his modeling, he demonstrated how he figured out unfamiliar words. He used his knowledge of prefixes, suffixes, roots, and context clues to decipher what words meant. For example, when he came to the word *cabinet,* he thought aloud, "Are they talking about kitchen cabinets? That's what I think about when I see the word *cabinet*. That can't be right. I can't believe that the author would be talking about George Washington's kitchen. But wait, there's a dash there, and when I read on it says, 'dash, the individuals who would head these departments and advise him.'" As part of his modeling, he came to the word *ratify,* and the book did not offer any context clues. He used his mobile phone to send a text message to a friend, who replied saying that *ratify* means to approve through the legal process.

Following the modeling, while students were working in groups and the teacher was meeting with four students who had struggled to explain their thinking on the exit slip the day before, a student asked what the word *progeny* meant. The teacher looked up to the larger group and asked, "Who has unlimited service and can look up *progeny* for Andrew?" Returning to the small group, he invited students to use Google images and search for the first Constitutional Convention. Looking at the various images they found, these students started talking with one another about the text they had been reading. They also asked questions of their teacher about the clothing they were seeing and the formality of the setting. During this conversation, the teacher noticed that one of his students was veering off track. Taking out his mobile phone, the teacher sent a quick text message to the student that read, "You okay? Need me?" Upon reading the message, the student looked over to the teacher, smiled, and went back to work.

Encouraging students to use current technology—to power up—allows them to interact with the curriculum and with one another in ways that teachers of the past could have only hoped for. When asked why they don't move from a power-down policy to a power-up policy, teachers and administrators report that they believe that students will abuse the policy and not focus on learning. Well, folks, students are already focused elsewhere. According to the Nielsen Telecom Practice Group, teens send 1,742 text messages per month (Covey, 2008). And *USA Today* reported that 25 percent of a teen's text messages are sent during class time (Toppo, 2009). In other words, prohibition policies aren't working. And further, these policies are not teaching students to be respectful. It is unlikely that the current power-down policies will result in a future community where adults refrain from talking on their phones at restaurants or in theaters.

Teaching Courtesy

Before teachers and schools can use technology for instruction, it seems reasonable to suggest that students must understand how to be respectful with the tools they have. Our experience suggests that focusing on a courtesy policy and teaching students the difference between courteous and discourteous behavior is an important prerequisite for 21st century learning. A sample courtesy policy, from our high school, can be found in figure 6.1. Of course, having a policy and teaching students what the policy means are two different things. The real key isn't the students; it's getting teachers to *teach* with this policy in place. It does no good to simply take away students' phones—that doesn't teach them how to use them respectfully. Rather, teachers need to talk with students and provide them feedback about the use of technology. At our school, it took several months and a lot of patience, but we're pleased to report that students now understand that they can use their technology for learning, and they are almost never disrespectful to teachers or peers. Gone are the days of teachers serving as police officers attempting to patrol the classroom for cell phones or MP3 players. And gone are the days of administrators having to discipline students about technology or having to collect phones to hold during the day.

Courtesy is a code that governs the expectations of social behavior. Each community or culture defines courtesy and the expectations for members of that community or culture. As a learning community, it is our responsibility to define courtesy and to live up to that definition. As a school community, we must hold ourselves and one another accountable for interactions that foster respect and trust. Discourteous behaviors destroy the community and can result in hurt feelings, anger, and additional poor choices.

In general, courtesy means that we interact with one another in positive, respectful ways. Consider the following examples of courteous and discourteous behavior.

Courteous	Discourteous
Saying please and thank you	Using vulgar, foul, abusive, or offensive language
Paying attention in class	
Socializing with friends during passing periods and lunch	Listening to an iPod during a formal learning situation such as during a lecture or while completing group work
Asking questions and interacting with peers and teachers	Text messaging or talking on a cell phone during class time
Asking for, accepting, offering, or declining help graciously	Bullying, teasing, or harassing others
Allowing teachers and peers to complete statements without interruptions	Hogging bandwidth and/or computer time
Throwing away trash after lunch	Not showing up for your scheduled appointments or completing tasks
Cleaning your own workspace	Failing to communicate when you're not coming to school
Reporting safety concerns or other issues that require attention to a staff member	

Figure 6.1: Sample courtesy policy.

This discussion brings us to a second challenge that must be addressed if schools are to move into the 21st century and develop students' skills with literacy 2.0.

Focus on Functions, not Forms

Technology can be overwhelming and discouraging if we let it be. Utilizing it does not require understanding the backend processes and complex sets of functions. At its heart, it is operated by one simple protocol: communication. In turn, our primary objective in using the technologies of today is to communicate, to get our point across loud and clear.

Eloquence, etiquette, fluency—these are all terms used to describe the persuasiveness, appropriateness, and clarity of one's message. The same terms apply to communication in technology.

Troubleshooting a technical problem starts with what is known. As a simple example, we know that a wired mouse plugs into a port on a computer. If this mouse stops working, what is the first step we take to solve the problem? We check the connection between the mouse and the computer, because we know this is how a mouse communicates with a computer. As a comparison, a student may need to create a book report with an image as the cover sheet. The student knows it is possible to type the report using an available word processing program but doesn't know how to add an image to the report. However, the student does know he can use his favorite search engine to ask "how to insert an image into a document." In return, the student will receive results that may include step-by-step instructions to fulfill his task. This combination of the student's purpose, the available tools, and the student's background knowledge of these tools helps produce the desired result.

Cybersafety

Once we have technology policies that reflect our beliefs and values, and teachers are comfortable with the technology, we are ready to address a third concern related to 21st century learning: cybersafety. The boogeyman of today lurks in the Internet, ready to pounce on children and take advantage of them. Who can forget the individual stories, such as the experiences of Katherine Tarbox (2004), one of the first victims of Internet predators?

Sadly, taking advantage of children didn't start with the Internet. The boogeyman of our childhood was waiting on the street corner ready to nab us from our bikes or driving by offering candy from a car. Yes, there are real risks that parents and children face, and schools must ensure that children are safe; it's our first, and primary, responsibility.

But along the way we have to be careful that we don't overstate the risk and accidentally prevent students from learning. In a study of the risks of online social networking, the National School Boards Association (2007) suggested that the Internet doesn't seem to be as dangerous as is often assumed. In their words, "Students and parents report fewer recent or current problems, such as cyberstalking, cyberbullying and unwelcome personal encounters, than school fears and policies seem to imply" (p. 5). Of the 1,277 nine- to seventeen-year-old students surveyed for the study, 20 percent reported seeing inappropriate images online, 18 percent reported seeing inappropriate language, 7 percent reported being asked for personal identifying information, 3 percent reported having unwelcome strangers try to communicate with them, 2 percent reported having a stranger ask them to meet in person, and .08 percent reported actually meeting someone in person without permission.

This group of students also told researchers about the other side of the Internet. Over half (59 percent) of them said that they regularly talked online about educational topics, such as going to college, politics, careers, religion, morals, ideas, and careers. In fact, 50 percent of the students said that they talked online about schoolwork.

Students online are more likely to be discussing school-related topics than engaging in behaviors that place them at risk. And we have to wonder whether those who do place themselves at risk would still be at risk even if they had *no* access to online interactions.

We were impressed by the work of Davis and McGrail (2009), who worked with fifth-graders to post blogs about classroom projects and current events. Students wrote about what they were reading, discussed school issues with students from Australia, and shared what they had learned about topics of individual interest. The authors noted that the issue of audience was essential to the students' learning. For this reason, they made a conscious decision to make the blog public. They didn't ignore the possible safety implications of this decision for their young students but felt that teaching them how to blog safely was far more useful than not allowing them to go public. The fifth-graders were taught about keeping personal information private and told that "if they received anything online that made them feel uncomfortable, they were to minimize their screens and immediately report concerns to the teacher" (p. 76). We have to feel that if ten-year-olds are capable of this work, why aren't we doing it more often with adolescents?

Future Tensions

Throughout this book we have attempted to define literacy 2.0 as a set of functions that parallel what humans have always done through spoken and written communication, and we have further expanded that definition as the ability to carry out these functions with an ever-growing set of tools. As educators, we are challenged to use these functions in new environments and with new tools, which of course creates new tensions as we shift our teaching practices to accommodate the changes.

Teacher educators Knobel and Wilber (2009) express a similar view when they write that "a Web 2.0 ethos values and promotes three interlocking functions or practices: participation, collaboration, and distribution" (p. 21). With that in mind, we gaze into a virtual crystal ball to make some predictions about the changes that are likely to occur around each of these functions in the second decade of the 21st century.

Participation: Digital Communication Will Continue to Transform Norms and Practices

During the summer of 2009, while we were writing this book, CNN published an online article titled "The 12 Most Annoying Types of Facebookers" (Griggs, 2009). The author listed the all-too-familiar violators, including the Let-Me-Tell-You-Everything-About-My-Day Bore, who feels the need to tell you about the peanut-butter-and-jelly sandwich she just ate, and the Chronic Inviter, who is constantly sending you invitations to join causes. One, the Self-Promoter, has earned his own slang term—Facebrag—because he is forever telling you about all the wonderful accomplishments of himself, his children, his dog . . .

As new means of communication develop, the norms for each evolve. When we first signed up for Facebook accounts, the expectations were unclear to us. As we "friended" people and were in turn friended by others, we acquired more experience at recognizing good and bad posts. As we wrote and read, we began to understand who the audience was and what the expectations were. It was a blissful day when we discovered we could hide the status reports on the games some of our friends played without having to shut those people out completely, something akin to changing the subject at a cocktail party.

Our point is not about Facebook per se, but about communication in general. As new technologies develop, a learner's understanding of audience must evolve as well. For those who use social networking, there are fine distinctions between the various platforms. As we write this, MySpace is the domain of younger adolescents, with older ones migrating to Facebook. Adults over thirty-five currently represent the fastest-growing segment on Facebook, leaving longtime members in the bewildering situation of having to explain Facebook to their parents (Facebook was originally conceived in 2004 by some Harvard University students as a way to communicate with one another and check out classmates). Many adults are further differentiating their personal and professional lives, using LinkedIn and Twitter for networking with colleagues.

As people increasingly represent themselves within a digital world, the social conventions and expectations of interpersonal communication will evolve. An oft-told story concerns Alexander Graham Bell and the invention of the telephone. On the heels of this new tool came the problem of how to answer it. Bell championed "Ahoy!" but this failed to catch on, and "Hello" became the standard greeting. Note that simply stating what the rules should be didn't work; the users decided. And so it is with every form of communication. Users determine the norms, and the savvy user detects the subtleties that signal the shifts. It will become increasingly important to be able to discern the voice behind the text and the visual representations (such as avatars) that people use to communicate who they are and what they value.

This has significant implications for education as well. As students interact more with those outside the walls of the classroom, their ability to represent themselves properly to the selected audience will play a larger role in curriculum and assessment. As noted in the previous chapter, being aware of audience is no longer simply about writing a paper with the teacher in mind. Audiences have expanded and require different levels of information. For instance, assigning a student to do research on influenza viruses will increasingly require that the information she shares be crafted for a variety of audiences. A blog, a tweet, a Wikipedia entry, a presentation for families of young children, and a podcast for schoolmates should be necessary aspects of the assignment. In addition, visual representations of information—graphs and tables, moving images, and a 60-second public service announcement—create further relevance for the research. The learning is no longer about telling the teacher what he already knows; it's about translating that information so that a host of audiences can benefit.

Collaboration: Massive Multiplayer Online Games Will Change Educational Practice

Many of us have a preconceived notion of online games. Young people, usually male, huddle in front of a glowing computer screen for hours on end, eschewing sunshine, green vegetables, and contact with other humans in the room. They live in a digital world where they slay monsters, wear funny clothes, and wreak virtual mayhem. Many of these so-called Massive Multiplayer Online (MMO) games do involve fantasy worlds and/or violent situations. Some, such as World of Warcraft (WoW), evolved out of computer and entertainment system games of the 1990s. Gamers meet online to construct characters (called avatars), build alliances, and fight battles (WoW had 11.5 million monthly subscribers in 2008). Kinder, gentler virtual worlds exist, of course.

One of the most familiar is Second Life, which is being used by a number of universities around the world to create classroom experiences. Second Life is also being used to support and extend existing media forms. Ira Flatow, host of *Science Friday* on National Public Radio, conducts his broadcasts simultaneously in Second Life and invites listeners to join him there.

Educational researchers and technology developers are teaming to create MMO experiences that can be used for learning. One of the more prominent developers in this emerging field is NASA, which is seeking partnerships with other developers to utilize NASA content in the MMO format to support science, technology, engineering, and math (STEM) fields. SimCity, another familiar game format since the 1980s, is now available as open-source code, which is allowing developers to create new games that allow children to build their own cities and interact with their citizens. And in what may be viewed with a mixture of awe and chagrin, a California company has announced the launch of an educational MMO for children ages three to ten that combines online learning games, virtual worlds, and social networking (www.jumpstart.com).

While it would be impossible to project where MMOs will go in the coming decade, what we want to consider are the functions they tap into. As we have stated throughout this book, emphasizing the tool at the expense of understanding the function stamps one's skills with an expiration date, because in no time a new tool will come along to replace it. The face of MMOs will change, but it is reasonable to expect that virtual collaborative worlds will be developed to foster learning. MMO environments combine many of the functions that we have discussed. Players create identities, join with others to accomplish tasks, search for information, and produce new knowledge. It will be vital for educators both to understand the appeal of these games to their students and to be knowledgeable about the ways good teaching can be applied to these contexts. Will classrooms of the future be virtual, with you as the teacher appearing only as an avatar?

Literacy researcher James Paul Gee (2007), whose work centers on communication, has devoted many years to understanding the value of games in learning. In particular, he cites the role of pleasure in learning and its benefits in heightening awareness and motivation. He also points out that the collaborative nature of games in an MMO environment elevates learning from a solitary event to one that is accomplished through what he calls "affinity groups." He explains that

> members of the affinity group have *extensive* knowledge. . . . By "extensive" I mean that members must be involved with many or all stages of the endeavor; able to carry out multiple, partly overlapping, functions; and able to reflect on the endeavor as a whole system, not just their part in it. Implication: No narrow specialists, no rigid roles. . . . In addition to extensive knowledge, members each have *intensive* knowledge—deep

and specialist knowledge in one or more areas. Members may well bring special intensive knowledge gained from their outside experiences and various sociocultural affiliations . . . to their affinity group's endeavors. Implication: Non-narrow specialists are good. (2007, p. 206)

We would add a bottom line to Gee's description of affinity groups—students must possess the skills and dispositions necessary to collaborate with one another. They can acquire them through cooperative learning tasks that result in productive group work. One doesn't need to sit in front of a screen in order to collaborate. Collaboration should occur every day, throughout the day, in the interactions created by thoughtful teachers who view learning as a co-constructed process that occurs in the company of others.

Distribution: Increased Access to Print and Visual Materials Will Alter Educational Expectations

Most of us have faced a security test while completing an online transaction. Such tests are designed to prevent breaches in the system, particularly spam (junk) email, automated blog postings, and other machine-based attacks. One popular type of security test enables a machine to determine whether there is really a human (and not another computer) on the other end of the transaction. An example you've probably encountered is the CAPTCHA, which requires you to type in a word that is shown in a distorted form and is therefore difficult for a computer to read. It's a pretty solid system and prevents many of the problems associated with automated programs that are designed to infiltrate other programs.

One of the inventors of CAPTCHA, Luis von Ahn, and his colleagues at Carnegie Mellon University have pointed the system in an ingenious new direction. Called reCAPTCHA, this project uses words from print materials that have proved difficult to digitize. Many of the physical books and texts printed before the 20th century not only suffer from deterioration but can be hard for machines to read because of the idiosyncratic spacing of handset types. People must transcribe words and phrases from these books, which can be a slow and expensive process. ReCAPTCHA takes these difficult words and places them in a security test so that when you enter the word, you are actually doing the human transcribing needed by the nonprofit Internet Archive to digitize books, newspapers, and other print materials. You'll recognize reCAPTCHA at work when you are asked to type in two words, rather than one (von Ahn, Mauer, McMillen, Abraham, & Blum, 2008). The motto of the reCAPTCHA Project (http://recaptcha.net) is "Digitizing Books One Word at a Time."

The breathtaking goal of the Internet Archive and Google Books is to make all print material available on the Web. This goal is as old as text itself, from the Ancient Library of Alexandria in the third century BCE, to the House of

Wisdom in ninth-century Babylon, to the U.S. Library of Congress, established in 1800. The lure of a single repository of knowledge is so strong that most organizations, large and small, spend time and money creating physical and digital records of the information they need for their endeavors. While it seems hard to imagine that such a goal could be accomplished, we have learned to expect the unexpected. And these anticipated changes will have a profound effect on educational expectations.

With the shift to increasingly digitized print and visual materials, learning will be transformed from a passive endeavor to an active one. Although the *tabula rasa* philosophy of children's learning has long since gone by the wayside, education up through the end of the 20th century often mirrored this belief, especially in positioning the teacher as the keeper of knowledge. An increased emphasis on standardized testing results in the last decade of the 20th century did little to dispel this practice, and even teachers who knew otherwise were made to feel as though a one-way transmission of knowledge could serve as a good proxy for learning. It cannot. As text- and image-based resources move online, learning will be less about regurgitating facts and more about finding, using, producing, and sharing information.

The position statements of the International Reading Association (IRA) and the National Council of Teachers of English (NCTE) reflect the sea change that had occurred in education by the end of the 20th century. We have already quoted the NCTE's 2009 list of the essential skills for 21st century literacy (see page 2). The IRA casts its statement in terms of the conditions students are entitled to if they are to "become proficient in the new literacies":

- Teachers who use ICTs [information and communications technologies] skillfully for teaching and learning effectively

- Peers who use ICTs responsibly and who share their knowledge

- A literacy curriculum that offers opportunities for collaboration with peers from around the world

- Instruction that embeds critical and culturally sensitive thinking into practice

- Standards and assessments that include new literacies

- Leaders and policymakers who are committed advocates of ICTs for teaching and learning

- Equal access to ICTs (International Reading Association, 2009)

Both of these literacy organizations recognize that the text-based literacies of reading and writing are more fully integrated into speaking, listening, and viewing than ever before. The privileging of text-based literacies at the expense of other elements of communication can no longer occur if students are to be truly prepared for their futures. It has been popular to bemoan the death of interpersonal communication in the digital age; we believe nothing could be further from the truth. What has occurred is that the functions of communication and literacy—sharing, storing, networking, presenting, producing, collaborating, and so on—have become infinitely more important with the expansion of the tools available to accomplish these tasks. As well, the text-based literacies of vocabulary, comprehension, fluency, and such are increasingly seen as essential to creating access to these digital tools. The result is higher—not lower—levels of literacy demand.

Living and Thriving in the 21st Century

Throughout this book we have attempted to make the case that literacy 2.0 represents sweeping changes in how we define a literate citizen and, therefore, what we do to educate him or her. There is no question that these changes cause stress that at times can be uncomfortable. It is likely that hard conversations will need to occur if we are to build an education system that can prepare students to craft a world for themselves that will be peaceful, productive, and inclusive. Teaching students how to find and evaluate information is hard. Making sure that students know how to collaborate with one another, be it across the table or across the world, is hard. Allowing students to produce and share, not just consume, knowledge is hard. It's much easier to remain in the comfort zone of what is familiar and continue to do what has always been done. And yet a central principle in education is that we prepare students for tomorrow, not just for today. Gandhi observed, "A principle is a principle, and in no case can it be watered down because of our incapacity to live it in practice. We have to strive to achieve it, and the striving should be conscious, deliberate, and hard." The difficulty of the task is no excuse for ignoring what needs to be done. Striving is thriving.

References

Alexie, S. (2007). *The absolutely true diary of a part-time Indian.* New York: Little, Brown.

American Library Association. (2008). *Fair use evaluator.* Accessed at http://librarycopyright.net/fairuse on February 11, 2010.

Anderson, L. W., & Krathwohl, D. R. (Eds.). (2001). *A taxonomy for learning, teaching, and assessing: A revision of Bloom's taxonomy of educational objectives.* New York: Longman.

Arledge, E., & Cort, J. (Writers/Producers). (2001). Cracking the code of life. [Television series episode]. In P. S. Apsell (Executive producer), *NOVA.* Accessed at www.pbs.org/wgbh/nova/genome/program_t.html on January 26, 2010.

Badke, W. (2007). *Plagiarism, eh? How to recognize it and get it out of your life.* Langley, BC, Canada: Trinity Western University Institutional Repository. Accessed at www.acts.twu.ca/Library/Plagiarism_Short.swf on January 26, 2010.

Barrows, H. S., & Tamblyn, R. M. (1980). *Problem-based learning: An approach to medical education.* New York: Springer.

Bass, W. (2009, January). Living authors are all around us. *English Journal, 98*(3), 13–14.

Benedict, T. (Producer/Director). (2004). *The conscientious objector* [Motion picture]. United States: Cinequest.

Bird, T. (1992). *American POWs of World War II: Forgotten men tell their stories.* London: Praeger.

Boyne, J. (2006). *The boy in the striped pajamas.* New York: David Fickling Books.

Britannica attacks . . . and we respond. (2006, March). *Nature, 440*(7084), 582. Accessed at www.nature.com/nature/journal/v440/n7084/pdf/440582b .pdf on February 11, 2010.

Burke, S., & Oomen-Early, J. (2008). That's blog worthy: Ten ways to integrate blogging into the health education classroom. *American Journal of Health Education, 39*(6), 362–364.

Carvell, M. (2002). *Who will tell my brother?* New York: Hyperion Books for Children.

Center for Social Media. (2008). *Code of best practices in fair use for media literacy education.* Accessed at www.centerforsocialmedia.org/resources/publications/ code_for_media_literacy_education on February 11, 2010.

Chandler, H. (2003, January). Concept mapping and WebQuests in social studies. *Media and Methods, 39*(3), 38–39.

Cooper, H., Robinson, J. C., & Patall, E. A. (2006). Does homework improve academic achievement? A synthesis of research, 1987–2003. *Review of Educational Research, 76*(1), 1–62.

Cornell University Law School. (2009). United States code collection: Title 17 §107. Limitations on exclusive rights: Fair use. *Copyright Law of the United States and Related Laws Contained in Title 17 of the United States Code.* Accessed at www4.law.cornell.edu/uscode/17/107.html on January 26, 2010.

Covey, N. (2008). Flying fingers. *Consumer Insight.* Accessed at http://en-us .nielsen.com/main/insights/consumer_insight/issue_12/flying_fingers on February 3, 2010.

Creative Commons. (2009). Creative commons: Share, remix, reuse—legally. Accessed at http://creativecommons.org/ on January 26, 2010.

Darth Tater. (2008, February 19). *Many voices on Darfur* [VoiceThread]. Accessed at http://ed.voicethread.com/#q.b62276.i322457 on January 28, 2010.

Davis, A. P., & McGrail, E. (2009, March). The joy of blogging. *Educational Leadership, 66*(6), 74–77.

Davis, S., Jenkins, G., & Hunt, R. (2002). *The pact: Three young men make a promise and fulfill a dream.* New York: Riverhead Books.

Dean, D. (2006). *Strategic writing: The writing process and beyond in the secondary English classroom.* Urbana, IL: National Council of Teachers of English.

Diamond Facts. (n.d.). In *Did You Know?* Accessed at http://didyouknow.org/ diamonds.htm on January 22, 2010.

Dodge, B. (1995, Summer). WebQuests: A technique for Internet-based learning. *Distance Educator, 1*(2), 10–13.

Doggett, L. (2009). *Nine great reasons why teachers should use twitter* [Blog]. Accessed at http://lauradoggett.com/2009/03/nine-great-reasons-why-teachers-should-use-twitter on January 27, 2010.

DomainTools. (2010). *Domain counts and Internet statistics.* Accessed at www.domaintools.com/internet-statistics on March 3, 2010.

Duke, N. K., & Pearson, P. D. (2002). Effective practices for developing reading comprehension. In A. E. Farstrup & S. J. Samuels (Eds.), *What research has to say about reading instruction* (3rd ed.) (pp. 205–242). Newark, DE: International Reading Association.

Dweeber. (2009, April). *About Dweeber.* Accessed at http://dweeber.com/Content.aspx?pid = 4 on February 8, 2010.

Ehrenreich, B. (2001). *Nickel and dimed: On (not) getting by in America.* New York: Henry Holt.

Eodice, M. (2008). Man bites dog: The public, the press, and plagiarism. In R. M. Howard & A. E. Robillard (Eds.), *Pluralizing plagiarism: Identities, contexts, pedagogies* (pp. 8–26**)**. Portsmouth, NH: Boynton/Cook.

Fisher, D., & Frey, N. (2001). *Responsive curriculum design in secondary schools: Meeting the diverse needs of students.* Lanham, MD: Scarecrow Education.

Fisher, D., & Frey, N. (2007a). *Checking for understanding: Formative assessments for your classroom.* Alexandria, VA: Association for Supervision and Curriculum Development.

Fisher, D., & Frey, N. (2007b). *Scaffolded writing instruction: Teaching with a gradual-release framework.* New York: Scholastic.

Fisher, D., & Frey, N. (2008a). *Better learning through structured teaching: A framework for the gradual release of responsibility.* Alexandria, VA: Association for Supervision and Curriculum Development.

Fisher, D., & Frey, N. (2008b). Homework and the gradual release of responsibility: Making "responsibility" possible. *English Journal, 98*(2), 40–45.

Fisher, D., & Frey, N. (2009). Feed up, back, forward. *Educational Leadership, 67*(3), 20–25.

Frey, N., & Fisher, D. (2006). *Language arts workshop: Purposeful reading and writing instruction.* Upper Saddle River, NJ: Pearson Merrill Prentice Hall.

Frey, N., Fisher, D., & Berkin, A. (2008). *Good habits, great readers: Building the literacy community.* Boston: Allyn and Bacon/Pearson.

Frey, N., Fisher, D., & Moore, K. (2009). Literacy letters: Comparative literature and formative assessment. *ALAN Review, 36*(2), 27–33.

Fullan, M., Hill, P., & Crévola, C. (2006). *Breakthrough.* Thousand Oaks, CA: Corwin Press.

Gee, J. P. (2007). *What video games have to teach us about learning and literacy* (Rev. ed.). New York: Palgrave Macmillan.

Giles, J. (2005). Internet encyclopaedias go head to head. *Nature, 438*(7070), 900–901. Accessed at http://obea.wikispaces/.com/file/view/nature_15dec 2005_wikipedia.pdf on February 11, 2010.

Gilmore, B. (2008). *Plagiarism: Why it happens, how to prevent it.* Portsmouth, NH: Heinemann.

Golding, W. (1959). *Lord of the flies.* New York: Capricorn Books.

Griggs, B. (2009, August 25). The 12 most annoying types of facebookers. *CNN .com/technology.* Accessed at www.cnn.com/2009/TECH/08/20/annoying .facebook.updaters/index.html on February 4, 2010.

Haddon, M. (2003). *The curious incident of the dog in the night-time.* New York: Doubleday.

Harris, C. (2009). Blogging from beyond the grave. *School Library Journal, 55*(4), 16.

Harris, R. (2007, June 15). Evaluating Internet research sources. *VirtualSalt.* Accessed at www.virtualsalt.com/evalu8it.htm on January 13, 2010.

Hess, D. E. (2009). *Controversy in the classroom: The democratic power of discussion.* New York: Routledge.

Hinchman, K. A., Alvermann, D. E., Boyd, F. B., Brozo, W. B., & Vacca, R. T. (2003). Supporting older students' in- and out-of-school literacies. *Journal of Adolescent and Adult Literacy, 47*(4), 304–310.

International Reading Association. (2009, May). *New literacies and 21st-century technologies: A position statement.* Accessed at www.reading.org/General/ AboutIRA/PositionStatements/21stCenturyLiteracies.aspx on February 5, 2010.

International Society for Technology in Education. (2007). *National educational technology standards for students.* Eugene, OR: Author. Accessed at www.iste.org/Content/NavigationMenu/NETS/ForStudents/NETS_for_ Students.htm on February 11, 2010.

Jackson, S. (2005). *The lottery and other stories* (2nd ed.). New York: Farrar, Straus and Giroux. (Original work published 1948)

Kass, L. R., & Wilson, J. Q. (1998). *The ethics of human cloning.* Washington, DC: AEI Press.

Kerr, M. E. (2001). *Slap your sides.* New York: HarperCollins.

Kinzie, S. (2008, August 10). An education in the dangers of online research. *Washington Post,* p. C5.

Knobel, M., & Wilber, D. (2009, March). Let's talk 2.0. *Educational Leadership, 66*(6), 20–24.

Kopcha, T. J. (2008, October 29). *WebQuest 101 part 1—What is a WebQuest?* [Video]. Accessed at www.youtube.com/watch?v = o4rel5qOPvU on February 9, 2010.

Krane, B. (2006, November 13). Researchers find kids need better online academic skills. *University of Connecticut Advance, 25(12).* Accessed at http://advance.uconn.edu/2006/061113/06111308.htm on March 1, 2010.

Lester, J. (2000). *To be a slave.* New York: Puffin.

Leu, D. J., Coiro, J., Castek, J., Hartman, D. K., Henry, L. A., & Reinking, D. (2008). Research on instruction and assessment in the new literacies of online reading comprehension. In C. C. Block & S. R. Paris (Eds.), *Comprehension instruction: Research-based best practices* (2nd ed.) (pp. 321–346). New York: Guilford.

Leu, D. J., O'Byrne, W. I., Zawilinski, L., McVerry, J. G., & Everett-Cacopardo, H. (2009). Expanding the new literacies conversation. *Educational Researcher, 38*(4), 264–269.

Levine, P., & Lopez, M. H. (2004, February). *Themes emphasized in social studies and civics classes: New evidence.* College Park, MD: Center for Information and Research on Civic Learning and Engagement. Accessed at www.civicyouth.org/PopUps/FactSheets/FS_Themes_Emphasized_SocStudies_Civics.pdf on February 11, 2010.

Lunsford, A. (2009, July). Literacy for life. *English Education, 41*(4), 396–397.

Machiavelli, N. (2007). *The prince: Machiavelli's description of the methods of murder adopted by Duke Valentino and the life of Castruccio Castracani* (W. K. Marriott, Trans.). Rockville, MD: Arc Manor. (Original work published 1532)

Margulies, P., & Rosaler, M. (2008). *The devil on trial: Witches, anarchists, atheists, communists, and terrorists in America's courtrooms.* Boston: Houghton Mifflin.

Markow, D., Kim, A., & Liebman, M. (2007). *The MetLife survey of the American teacher: The homework experience.* New York: Metropolitan Life

Insurance Company. Accessed at http://www.eric.ed.gov/ERICDocs/data/ericdocs2sql/content_storage_01/0000019b/80/3c/f3/74.pdf on February 8, 2010.

McDonald, J. E. R. (2008). Podcasting a physics lecture. *The Physics Teacher, 46*(8), 490–493.

McKenzie, J. (2007, June 4). *Before he cheats* [Video]. Accessed at www.youtube.com/watch?v = 5NvA4hCOfjU&feature = related on January 22, 2010.

McNulty, S. (2009). *Building a WordPress blog people want to read.* Berkeley, CA: Peachpit Press.

Meisel, M. S. (2007, April 27). The public genome: Cheap sequencing technology will let you—and maybe the world—see your DNA. *The Harvard Crimson Online Edition.* Accessed at www.thecrimson.com/article.aspx?ref = 518564 on February 11, 2010.

National Council of Teachers of English. (2008, November). *NCTE position statement: 21st century curriculum and assessment framework.* Accessed at http://www.ncte.org/positions/statements/21stcentframework on February 5, 2010.

National Council of Teachers of English. (2009, March). Literacy learning in the 21st century: A policy brief produced by the National Council of Teachers of English. *Council Chronicle, 18*(3), 15–16.

National Public Radio. (n.d.). *NPR community discussion rules.* Accessed at www.npr.org/help/discussionrules.html on January 27, 2010.

National School Boards Association. (2007, July). *Creating and connecting: Research and guidelines on online social—and educational—networking.* Alexandria, VA: Author.

Nelson, P. (2002). *Left for dead: A young man's search for justice for the USS Indianapolis.* New York: Delacorte Press.

Nowak, J. (2008, June 5). Circleville valedictorian steps down after admitting he plagiarized commencement speech. *The Columbus Dispatch.* Accessed at www.dispatch.com/live/content/local_news/stories/2008/06/05/plagiarism.html?print = yes&sid = 101 on February 11, 2010.

Ohler, J. (2009, March). Orchestrating the media collage. *Educational Leadership, 66*(6), 8–13.

Orwell, G. (2003). *1984.* New York: Plume. (Original work published 1949)

Pak, M. (2009, February). Podcasting: Scaffolding conceptual understanding in writing. *California English, 14*(3), 20–23.

PBS. (2008, June 29). *NOVA scienceNOW: Personal Genome Project.* [Video]. Accessed at www.youtube.com/watch?v = MjevOzSHZTU on January 26, 2010.

Pelzer, D. J. (1993). *A child called it.* Omaha, NE: Omaha Press.

Pichert, J. W., & Anderson, R. C. (1977). Taking different perspectives on a story. *Journal of Educational Psychology, 69,* 309–315.

Plagiarism. (2010, January 21). *Wikipedia.* Accessed at http://en.wikipedia .org/wiki/Plagiarism on January 22, 2010.

Podcast. (2010, January 23). *Wikipedia.* Accessed at http://en.wikipedia.org/ wiki/Podcast on January 25, 2010.

Powell, J. (2002). *The Julie/Julia project* [Blog]. Accessed at blogs.salon.com/ 0001399/2002/08/25.html on January 27, 2010.

Powell, J. (2005). *Julie and Julia: 365 days, 524 recipes, 1 tiny apartment kitchen.* New York: Little, Brown.

Prensky, M. (2008, November). *Homo Sapiens Digital: Technology is their birth-right.* Keynote presentation at the annual meeting of the National Council of Teachers of English, San Antonio, TX.

Puccinelli, M. (2008, May 29). Naperville H.S. principal fired for plagiarism. *CBS 2 News, Chicago* [Television broadcast]. Accessed at http://cbs2chicago .com/local/naperville.principal.plagiarism.2.736184.html on August 13, 2008.

Rosenblatt, L. M. (1994). *The reader, the text, the poem: The transactional theory of the literary work.* Carbondale, IL: Southern Illinois University Press. (Original work published 1938)

Rosoff, M. (2004). *How I live now.* New York: Wendy Lamb Books.

Santa, C. M, & Havens, L. T. (1995). *Project CRISS: Creating independence through student-owned strategies.* Dubuque, IA: Kendall/Hunt.

Satrapi, M. (2003). *Persepolis: The story of a childhood.* New York: Pantheon.

SayUncle. (2006). *The perils of three-dimensional reading* [Blog]. Accessed at www.saysuncle.com/archives/2002/09/06/the-perils-of-three-dimensional-reading on January 8, 2010.

Scanlon, J. H., & Wieners, B. (1999, July 9). The Internet cloud. *The Original Industry Standard Archive.* Accessed at www.thestandard.com/article/ 0,1902,5466,00.html on February 11, 2010.

Silenticeriver. (2008, January 5). *Duran Duran Second Life machinisma mashup* [Video]. Accessed at www.youtube.com/watch?v = 1Hi8fPVNreg on January 28, 1010.

Speak Up. (2009, March 24). *Speak up 2008 congressional briefing.* Accessed at www.tomorrow.org/speakup/speakup_congress.html on April 5, 2009.

Spinelli, J. (2004). *Wringer.* New York: HarperTeen.

Tan, A. (2006). *The joy luck club.* New York: Penguin. (Original work published 1989)

Tarbox, K. (2004). *A girl's life online.* New York: Plume.

Tasmania Department of Education. (2007). *English learning area: Critical literacy.* Accessed at wwwfp.education.tas.gov.au/English/critlit.htm on January 20, 2010.

Toppo, G. (2009, June 17). Survey: Many teens use phones in class to text or cheat. *USA Today.* Accessed at www.usatoday.com/news/education/2009-06-17-cellphones-in-class_N.htm on March 3, 2010.

Trier, J. (2007, February). "Cool" engagements with YouTube: Part 1. *Journal of Adolescent & Adult Literacy, 50*(5), 408–412.

University of Leeds. (n.d.). *Teaching resources: Plagiarism game.* Accessed at www.lts.leeds.ac.uk/plagiarism/teaching.php#game on January 29, 2010.

University of Pennsylvania. (2008, June). *Steps in making a video mashup.* Accessed at http://wic.library.upenn.edu/multimedia/tutorials/mashup.html on February 11, 2010.

University of Washington. (2005–2008). *AccessIT web design and development I.* Accessed at www.washington.edu/accessit/webdesign/index.htm on February 11, 2010.

Von Ahn, L., Mauer, B., McMillen, C., Abraham, D., & Blum, M. (2008, September). reCAPTCHA: Human-based character recognition via web security measures. *Science, 321*(5895), 1465–1468.

Vosen, M. A. (2008). Using Bloom's taxonomy to teach students about plagiarism. *English Journal, 97*(6), 43–46.

Warschauer, M. (2003). *Technology and social inclusion: Rethinking the digital divide.* Cambridge, MA: MIT Press.

Waters, D. (2008). *Generation dead.* New York: Hyperion.

Weiser, M. (1991). The computer for the 21st century. *Scientific American, 265*(3), 94–104.

Wells, H. G. (1995). *The Time Machine.* Mineola, NY: Dover Publications. (Original work published 1895)

WestEd. (2009, July 24). *Technological literacy framework for the 2012 National Assessment of Educational Progress: Discussion draft.* Accessed at http://www.edgateway.net/cs/naepsci/print/docs/470 on February 11, 2010.

Wiggins, G., & McTighe, J. (2005). *Understanding by design* (2nd ed.). Alexandria, VA: Association for Supervision and Curriculum Development.

Wollman-Bonilla, J. E. (2001, April). Can first-grade writers demonstrate audience awareness? *Reading Research Quarterly, 36*(2), 184–201.

Index